WARWICK
The Kingmaker

Charles W. Oman

Originally published in 1891

TABLE OF CONTENTS

Chapter 1
THE DAYS OF THE KINGMAKER

Chapter 2
THE HOUSE OF NEVILLE

Chapter 3
RICHARD OF SALISBURY

Chapter 4
THE KINGMAKER'S YOUTH

Chapter 5
THE CAUSE OF YORK

Chapter 6
THE BEGINNING OF THE CIVIL WAR: ST. ALBANS

Chapter 7
WARWICK CAPTAIN OF CALAIS AND ADMIRAL

Chapter 8
WARWICK IN EXILE

Chapter 9
VICTORY AND DISASTER—NORTHAMPTON AND ST. ALBANS

Chapter 10
TOWTON FIELD

Chapter 11
THE TRIUMPH OF KING EDWARD

Chapter 12
THE PACIFICATION OF THE NORTH

Chapter 13
THE QUARREL OF WARWICK AND KING EDWARD

Chapter 14
PLAYING WITH TREASON

Chapter 15
WARWICK FOR KING HENRY

Chapter 16
THE RETURN OF KING EDWARD

Chapter 17
BARNET

Chapter 1

THE DAYS OF THE KINGMAKER

Of all the great men of action who since the Conquest have guided the course of English policy, it is probable that none is less known to the reader of history than Richard Neville Earl of Warwick and Salisbury. The only man of anything approaching his eminence who has been treated with an equal neglect is Thomas Cromwell, and of late years the great minister of Henry the Eighth is beginning to receive some of the attention that is his due. But for the Kingmaker, the man who for ten years was the first subject of the English Crown, and whose figure looms out with a vague grandeur even through the misty annals of the Wars of the Roses, no writer has spared a monograph. Every one, it is true, knows his name, but his personal identity is quite ungrasped. Nine persons out of ten if asked to sketch his character would find, to their own surprise, that they were falling back for their information to Lord Lytton's Last of the Barons or Shakespeare's Henry the Sixth.

An attempt, therefore, even an inadequate attempt, to trace out with accuracy his career and his habits of mind from the original authorities cannot fail to be of some use to the general reader as well as to the student of history. The result will perhaps appear meagre to those who are accustomed to the biographies of the men of later centuries. We are curiously ignorant of many of the facts that should aid us to build up a picture of the man. No trustworthy representation of his bodily form exists. The day of portraits was not yet come; his monument in Bisham Abbey has long been swept away; no writer has even deigned to describe his personal appearance—we know not if he was dark or fair, stout or slim. At most we may gather from the vague phrases of the chroniclers, and from his quaint armed figure in the Rous Roll, that he was of great stature and breadth of limb. But perhaps the good Rous was thinking of his fame rather than his body, when he sketched the Earl in that quaint pictorial pedigree over-topping all his race save his cousin and king and enemy, Edward the Fourth.

But Warwick has only shared the fate of all his contemporaries. The men of the fifteenth century are far less well known to us than are their grandfathers or their grandsons. In the fourteenth century the chroniclers were still working on their old scale; in the sixteenth the literary spirit had descended on the whole nation, and great men and small were writing hard at history as at every other branch of knowledge. But in the days of Lancaster and York the old fountains had run dry, and the new flood of the Renaissance had not risen. The materials for reconstructing history are both scanty and hard to handle. We dare not swallow Hall and Hollingshead whole, as was the custom for two hundred years, or take their annals, coloured from end to end with Tudor sympathies, as good authority for the doings of the previous century. Yet when we have put aside their fascinating, if somewhat untrustworthy, volumes, we find ourselves wandering in a very dreary waste of fragments and scraps of history, strung together on the meagre thread of two or three dry and jejune compilations of annals. To have to take William of Worcester or good Abbot Whethamsted as the groundwork of a continuous account of the times is absolutely maddening. Hence it comes to pass that Warwick has failed to receive his dues.

Of all the men of Warwick's century there are only two whose characters we seem thoroughly to grasp—the best and the worst products of the age—Henry the Fifth and Richard the Third. The achievements of the one stirred even the feeble writers of that day into a fulness of detail in which they indulge for no other hero; the other served as the text for so many invectives under the Tudors that we imagine that we see a real man in the gloomy portrait that is set up before us. Yet we may fairly ask whether our impression is not drawn, either at first or at second hand, almost entirely from Sir Thomas More's famous biography of the usurper, a work whose literary merits have caused it to be received as the only serious source for Richard's history. If we had not that work, Richard of Gloucester would seem a vaguely-defined monster of iniquity, as great a puzzle to the student of history as are the other shadowy forms which move on through those evil times to fall, one after the other, into the bloody grave which was the common lot of all.

In spite, however, of the dearth of good chronicles, and of the absolute non-existence of any contemporary writers of literary merit, there are authorities enough of one sort and another to make it both possible and profitable to build up a detailed picture of Warwick and his times. First and foremost, of course, come the invaluable Paston Letters, covering the whole period, and often supplying the vivid touches of detail in which the more formal documents are so lamentably deficient. If but half a dozen families, as constant in letter-writing as John and Margery Paston, had transmitted their correspondence to posterity, there would be little need to grumble at our lack of information. Other letters too exist, scattered in collections, such as the interesting scrawl from Warwick himself, in his dire extremity before Barnet fight, to Henry Vernon, which was turned up a year ago among the lumber at Belvoir Castle. Much can be gathered from rolls and inquests—for example, the all-important information as to centres and sources of local power can be traced out with perfect accuracy from the columns of the Escheats Roll, where each peer or knight's lands are carefully set forth at the moment of his decease. Joining one authority to another, we may fairly build up the England of the fifteenth century before our eyes with some approach to completeness.

The whole picture of the times is very depressing on the moral if not on the material side. There are few more pitiful episodes in history than the whole tale of the reign of Henry the Sixth, the most unselfish and well-intentioned king that ever sat upon the English throne—a man of whom not even his enemies and oppressors could find an evil word to say; the troubles came, as they confessed, "all because of his false lords, and never of him." We feel that there must have been something wrong with the heart of a nation that could see unmoved the meek and holy King torn from wife and child, sent to wander in disguise up and down the kingdom for which he had done his poor best, and finally doomed to pine for five years a prisoner in the fortress where he had so long held his royal Court. Nor is our first impression concerning the demoralisation of England wrong. Every line that we read bears home to us more and more the fact that the nation had fallen on evil times. First and foremost among the causes of its moral deterioration was the wretched French War, a war begun in the pure spirit of greed and ambition,—there was not even the poor excuse that had existed in the time of Edward the Third—carried on by the aid of hordes of debauched foreign mercenaries (after Henry the Fifth's death the native English seldom formed more than a third of any host that took the field in France), and persisted in long after it had become hopeless, partly from misplaced national pride, partly because of the personal interests of the ruling classes. Thirty-five years of a war that was as unjust as it was unfortunate had both soured and demoralised the nation. England was full of disbanded soldiers of fortune; of knights who had lost the ill-gotten lands across the Channel, where they had maintained a precarious lordship in the days of better fortune; of castellans and governors whose occupation was gone; of hangers-on of all sorts who had once maintained themselves on the spoils of Normandy and Guienne. Year after year men and money had been lavished on the war to no effect; and when the final catastrophe came, and the fights of Formigny and Chatillon ended the chapter of our disasters, the nation began to cast about for a scapegoat on whom to lay the burden of its failures. The real blame lay on the nation itself, not on any individual; and the real fault that had been committed was not the mismanagement of an enterprise which presented any hopes of success, but a wrong-headed persistence in an attempt to conquer a country which was too strong to be held down. However, the majority of the English people chose to assume firstly that the war with France might have been conducted to a prosperous issue, and secondly that certain particular persons were responsible for its having come to the opposite conclusion. At first the unfortunate Suffolk and Somerset had the responsibility laid upon them. A little later the outcry became more bold and fixed upon the Lancastrian dynasty itself as being to blame not only for disaster abroad, but for the "want of governance" at home. If King Henry had understood the charge, and possessed the wit to answer it, he might fairly have replied that his subjects must fit the burden upon their own backs, not upon his. The war had been weakly conducted, it was true; but weakly because the men and money for it were grudged. The England that could put one hundred thousand men into the field in a civil broil at Towton sent four thousand to fight the decisive battle at Formigny that settled our fate in Normandy. At home the bulwarks of social order seemed crumbling away. Private wars, riot, open highway robbery, murder, abduction, armed resistance to the law, prevailed on a scale that had been unknown since the troublous times of Edward the Second—we might almost say since the evil days of Stephen. But it was not the Crown alone that should have been blamed for the state of the realm. The nation had chosen to impose over-stringent constitutional checks on the kingly power before it was ripe for self-government, and the Lancastrian house sat on the throne because it had agreed to submit to those checks. If the result of the experiment was disastrous, both parties to the contract had to bear their share of the responsibility. But a nation seldom allows that it has been wrong; and Henry of Windsor had to serve as scapegoat for all the misfortunes of the realm, because Henry of Bolingbroke had committed his descendants to the unhappy compact.

Want of a strong central government was undoubtedly the complaint under which England was labouring in the middle of the fifteenth century, and all the grievances against which outcry was made were but symptoms of one latent disease.

Ever since the death of Henry the Fifth the internal government of the country had been steadily going from bad to worse. The mischief had begun in the young King's earliest years. The Council of Regency that ruled in his name had from the first proved unable to make its authority felt as a single individual ruler might have done. With the burden of the interminable French War weighing upon their backs, and the divisions caused by the quarrels of Beaufort and Gloucester dividing them into factions, the councillors had not enough attention to spare for home government. As early as 1428 we find them, when confronted by the outbreak of a private war in the north, endeavouring to patch up the quarrel by arbitration, instead of punishing the offenders on each side. Accounts of riotous assemblages in all parts of the country, of armed violence at parliamentary elections, of party fights in London at Parliament time—like that which won for the meeting of 1426 the name of the Parliament of Bats (bludgeons)—grow more and more common. We even find treasonable insurrection appearing in the strange obscure rising of the political Lollards under Jack Sharp in 1431, an incident which shows how England was on the verge of bloodshed twenty years before the final outbreak of civil war was to take place.

But all these public troubles would have been of comparatively small importance if the heart of the nation had been sound. The phenomenon which makes the time so depressing is the terrible decay in private morals since the previous century. A steady deterioration is going on through the whole period, till at its end we find hardly a single individual in whom it is possible to interest ourselves, save an occasional Colet or Caxton, who belongs in spirit, if not date, to the oncoming renascence of the next century. There is no class or caste in England which comes well out of the scrutiny. The Church, which had served as the conscience of the nation in better times, had become dead to spiritual things; it no longer produced either men of saintly life or learned theologians or patriotic statesmen. In its corporate capacity it had grown inertly orthodox. Destitute of any pretence of spiritual energy, yet showing a spirit of persecution such as it had never displayed in earlier centuries, its sole activity consisted in hunting to the stake the few men who displayed any symptoms of thinking for themselves in matters of religion. So great was the deadness of the Church that it was possible to fall into trouble, like Bishop Pecock, not for defending Lollardry, but for showing too much originality in attacking it. Individually the leading churchmen of the day were politicians and nothing more, nor were they as a rule politicians of the better sort; for one like Beaufort, who was at any rate consistent and steadfast, there are many Bourchiers and George Nevilles and Beauchamps, who merely sailed with the wind and intrigued for their own fortunes or those of their families.

Of the English baronage of the fifteenth century we shall have so much to say in future chapters that we need not here enlarge on its characteristics. Grown too few and too powerful, divided into a few rival groups, whose political attitude was settled by a consideration of family grudges and interests rather than by any grounds of principle, or patriotism, or loyalty, they were as unlike their ancestors of the days of John or Edward the First as their ecclesiastical contemporaries were unlike Langton or even Winchelsey. The baronage of England had often been unruly, but it had never before developed the two vices which distinguished it in the times of the Two Roses—a taste for indiscriminate bloodshed and a turn for rapid political apostasy. To put prisoners to death by torture as did Tiptoft Earl of Worcester, to desert to the enemy in the midst of battle like Lord Grey de Ruthyn at Northampton, or Stanley at Bosworth, had never before been the custom of England. It is impossible not to recognise in such traits the results of the French War. Twenty years spent in contact with French factions, and in command of the godless mercenaries who formed the bulk of the English armies, had taught our nobles lessons of cruelty and faithlessness such as they had not before imbibed. Their demoralisation had been displayed in France long ere the outbreak of civil war caused it to manifest itself at home.

But if the Church was effete and the baronage demoralised, it might have been thought that England should have found salvation in the sound heartedness of her gentry and her burgesses. Unfortunately such was not to be the case. Both of these classes were growing in strength and importance during the century, but when the times of trouble came they gave no signs of aspiring to direct the destinies of the nation. The House of Commons which should, as representing those classes, have gone on developing its privileges, was, on the contrary, thrice as important in the reign of Henry the Fourth as in that of Edward the Fourth. The knights and squires showed on a smaller scale all of the vices of the nobility.

Instead of holding together and maintaining a united loyalty to the Crown, they bound themselves by solemn sealed bonds and the reception of "liveries" each to the baron whom he preferred. This fatal system, by which the smaller landholder agreed on behalf of himself and his tenants to follow his greater neighbour in peace and war, had ruined the military system of England, and was quite as dangerous as the ancient feudalism. The salutary old usage, by which all freemen who were not tenants of a lord served under the sheriff in war, and not under the banner of any of the baronage, had long been forgotten. Now, if all the gentry of a county were bound by these voluntary indentures to serve some great lord, there was no national force in that county on which the Crown could count, for the yeoman followed the knight as the knight followed the baron. If the gentry constituted themselves the voluntary followers of the baronage, and aided their employers to keep England unhappy, the class of citizens and burgesses took a very different line of conduct. If not actively mischievous, they were sordidly inert. They refused to entangle themselves in politics at all. They submitted impassively to each ruler in turn, when they had ascertained that their own persons and property were not endangered by so doing. A town, it has been remarked, seldom or never stood a siege during the Wars of the Roses, for no town ever refused to open its gates to any commander with an adequate force who asked for entrance. If we find a few exceptions to the rule, we almost always learn that entrance was denied not by the citizens, but by some garrison of the opposite side which was already within the walls. Loyalty seems to have been as wanting among the citizens as among the barons of England. If they generally showed some slight preference for York rather than for Lancaster, it was not on any moral or sentimental ground, but because the house of Lancaster was known by experience to be weak in enforcing "good governance," and the house of York was pledged to restore the strength of the Crown and to secure better times for trade than its rival.

Warwick was a strong man, born at the commencement of Henry the Sixth's unhappy minority, whose coming of age coincided with the outburst of national rage caused by the end of the disastrous French War, whose birth placed him at the head of one of the great factions in the nobility, whose strength of body and mind enabled him to turn that headship to full account. How he dealt with the problems which inevitable necessity laid before him we shall endeavour to relate.

Charles W. Oman

Chapter 2

THE HOUSE OF NEVILLE

Of all the great houses of medieval England, the Nevilles of Raby were incontestably the toughest and the most prolific. From the reign of John to the reign of Elizabeth their heritage never once passed into the female line, and in all the fourteen generations which lived and died between 1210 and 1600 there was only one occasion on which the succession passed from uncle to nephew, and not from father to son or grandson. The vitality of the Neville tribe was sufficient to bear them through repeated marriages with those only daughters and heiresses whose wedlock so often forebodes the extinction of an ancient house. Of four successive heads of the family between 1250 and 1350, all married ladies who were the last representatives of old baronial houses; but the Nevilles only grew more numerous, and spread into more and more branches, extending their possessions farther and farther from their original seat on the Durham moors till all the counties of the north were full of their manors.

The original source of the family was a certain Robert Fitz-Maldred, lord of Raby, who, in the reign of John, married Isabella de Neville, heiress of his neighbour Geoffrey de Neville of Brancepeth. Robert's son Geoffrey, who united the Teesdale lands of his father with his mother's heritage hard by the gates of Durham, took the name of Neville, and that of Fitz-Maldred was never again heard in the family. The lords of Raby did not at first distinguish themselves in any way above the rest of the barons of the North Country. We find them from time to time going forth to the King's Scotch or French wars, serving in Simon de Montfort's rebel army, wrangling with their feudal superior the Bishop of Durham, slaying an occasional sheriff, and founding an occasional chantry, and otherwise conducting themselves after the manner of their kind. It was one of the house who led the English van against the Scots at the great victory of 1346, and erected the graceful monument which gave to the battlefield the name of Neville's Cross.

Only two characteristics marked these Nevilles of the thirteenth and fourteenth centuries; the largeness of their families—three successive lords of Raby boasted respectively of ten, eleven, and nine children—and their never-ending success in laying field by field and manor by manor. Robert Neville, who in the time of Henry the Third married Ida Mitford, added to his Durham lands his wife's broad Northumbrian barony in the valley of the Wansbeck. His son of the same name made Neville one of the greatest names in Yorkshire, when he wedded Mary of Middleham, and became in her right lord of Middleham Castle and all the manors dependent on it, reaching for a dozen miles along the Ure and running up to the farthest bounds of the forest of Coverdale. Robert the younger's heir, Ralph, emulated the good fortune of his father and grandfather by securing as his wife Euphemia, heiress of Clavering, who brought him not only the half-hundred of Clavering in Essex, but the less remote and more valuable lands of Warkworth on the Northumbrian coast. Ralph's son John, though he married as his first wife a younger daughter of the house of Percy, secured as his second Elizabeth Latimer, heiress of an old baronial house whose domains lay scattered about Bucks and Bedfordshire.

Four generations of wealthy marriages had made the Nevilles the greatest lords in all the North Country. Even their neighbours, the Percies of Northumberland, were not so strong. The "saltire argent on the field gules," and the dun bull, the two Neville badges, were borne by hosts of retainers. Three hundred men-at-arms, of whom fourteen were knights and three hundred archers, followed the lord of Raby even when he went so far afield as Brittany. For home service against the Scots he could muster thrice as many. More than seventy manors were in his hands, some spread far and wide in Essex, Norfolk, Bedfordshire, and Buckinghamshire, but the great bulk of them lying massed in North Yorkshire and South Durham, around Raby and Middleham, the two strong castles which were the centres of his influence. Hence it was not surprising that King Richard the Second, when he lavished titles and honours broadcast on the nobility after his surprising coup d'état of 1397, should have singled out the head of the Nevilles for conciliation and preferment. Accordingly, Ralph Neville, then in the thirty-fourth year of his age, was raised to the dignity of an earl. Curiously enough, he could not be given the designation of either of the counties where the bulk of his broad lands lay. The earldom of Durham was, now as always, in the hands of its bishop, comes palatinus of the county since the days of William the Conqueror. The titles of York and of Richmondshire, wherein lay the other great stretch of Neville land, were vested in members of the royal house. The Percies had twenty years before received the title of Northumberland, the third county where the Nevilles held considerable property. Hence Ralph of Raby had to be put off with the title of Westmoreland, though in that county he seems, curiously enough, not to have held a single manor. The gift of the earldom was accompanied with the more tangible present of the royal honour of Penrith.

All these favours, however, did not buy the loyalty of Ralph Neville. He was married to one of John of Gaunt's daughters by Katherine Swinford, and was at heart a strong partisan of the house of Lancaster. Accordingly, when Henry of Bolingbroke landed at Ravenspur in July 1399, Westmoreland was one of the first to join him; he rode with him to Flint, saw the surrender of King Richard, and bore the royal sceptre at the usurper's coronation at Westminster. Henry rewarded his services by making him Earl Marshal in place of the exiled Duke of Norfolk.

Earl Ralph went on in a prosperous career, aided King Henry against the rising of the Percies in 1403, and committed himself more firmly than ever to the cause of the house of Lancaster by putting down the insurrection which Scrope, Mowbray, and the aged Northumberland had raised in 1405. Twice he served King Henry as ambassador to treat with the Scots, and twice the custody of the Border was committed to him as warden. When Bolingbroke died, and Henry of Monmouth succeeded him, Earl Ralph was no less firm and faithful. At the famous Parliament of Leicester in 1414, when the glorious but fatal war with France was resolved upon, he was one of the few who withstood the arguments of Archbishop Chicheley and the appeals of the Duke of Exeter and gave their voices against the expedition. He besought the King that, if he must needs make war, he should attack Scotland rather than France, the English title to that crown being as good, the enterprise more hopeful, and the result more likely to bring permanent profit, while—quoting an old popular rhyme—he ended by saying that

He that wolde France win, must with Scotland first begin.

But all men cried "War! War! France! France!" The ambitious young King had his will; and the next spring there sailed from Southampton the first of those many gallant hosts of Englishmen who were to win so many fruitless battles to their country's final loss, and leave their bones behind to moulder in French soil, in the trenches of Harfleur and Orleans or on the fields of Beaugé and Patay.

Every reader of Shakespeare has met Earl Ralph in the English camp on the eve of the battle of Agincourt, remembers his downhearted wish for a few thousands of the "gentlemen of England now abed," and can repeat by heart the young King's stirring reply to his uncle's forebodings. But, in fact, Earl Ralph was not at Agincourt, nor did he even cross the sea. He had been left behind with Lord Scrope and the Baron of Greystock to keep the Scottish March, and was far away at Carlisle when Henry's little band of English were waiting for the dawn on that eventful St. Crispin's day. Unless tradition errs, it was really Walter of Hungerford who made the speech that drew down his master's chiding.

Ralph was now growing an old man as the men of the fifteenth century reckoned old age; and while the brilliant campaigns of Henry the Fifth were in progress abode at home, busied with statecraft rather than with war. But his sons, and they were a numerous tribe, were one after another sent across the seas to join their royal cousin. John, the heir of Westmoreland, was serving all through the campaigns of 1417-18, and was made governor of Verneuil and other places in its neighbourhood, after having held the trenches opposite the Porte de Normandie during the long siege of Rouen, and assisted also at the leaguer of Caen. Ralph, Richard, William, and George are found following in their elder brother's footsteps as each of them arrived at the years of manhood, and all earned their knighthood by services done in France.

Meanwhile Earl Ralph, after surviving his royal nephew some three years, and serving for a few months as one of the Privy Council that governed in the name of the infant Henry the Sixth, died on October 21st, 1425, at the age of sixty-two, and was buried in the beautiful collegiate church which he had founded at Staindrop, hard by the gates of his ancestral castle of Raby. There his monument still remains, escaped by good fortune from the vandalism of Edwardian and Cromwellian Protestants. He lies in full armour, wearing the peaked basinet that was customary in his younger days, though it had gone out of fashion ere his death. His regular features have little trace of real portraiture, and show no signs of his advancing years, so that we may conclude that the sculptor had never been acquainted with the man he was representing. Only the short twisted moustache, curling over the mail of the Earl's camail, has something of individuality, and must have corresponded to the life; for by 1425 all the men of the younger generation were close shaven, like King Henry the Fifth. On Earl Ralph's right hand, as befitted a princess of the blood royal, lies his second wife Joan of Beaufort; on his left Margaret Stafford, the bride of his youth and the mother of his heir.

Charles W. Oman

Chapter 3

RICHARD OF SALISBURY

Earl Ralph, surpassing all his keen and prolific ancestors not only in the success with which he pushed his fortunes, but in the enormous family which he reared, had become the father of no less than twenty-three children by his two wives. Nine were the offspring of Margaret of Stafford, fourteen of Joan of Beaufort. John, the heir of Westmoreland, had died a few years before his father, and the earldom passed to his son, Ralph the second, now a lad of about eighteen. But the greater number of the other twenty-two children still survived, and their fortunes influenced the after history both of the house of Neville and the kingdom of England to such an extent that they need careful statement.

The old Earl had turned all his energies into negotiating the marriages of his children, and partly by the favour of the two Henries, partly by judicious buying up of wardships in accordance with the practice of the fifteenth century, partly by playing on the desire of his neighbours to be allied to the greatest house of the North Country, he had succeeded in establishing a compact family group, which was already by 1425 one of the factors to be reckoned with in English politics. The most important of these connections by far was the wedding of his youngest daughter Cecily to Richard Duke of York—a marriage brought about by royal favour shortly before the Earl's death, while both the contracting parties were mere children; the Duke some eleven years old, the little bride about nine.[1] By this union Ralph of

Westmoreland was destined to become the ancestor of a score of kings and queens of England. It bound the house of Neville to the Yorkist cause, and led away the children of Ralph from that loyalty to Lancaster which had been the cause of their father's greatness. But at the time when the marriage was brought about no one could well have foreseen the Wars of the Roses, and we may acquit the Earl of any design greater than that of increasing the prosperity of his house by another marriage with a younger branch of the royal stock. His own union with Joan of Beaufort had served him so well, that he could desire nothing better for the next generation. The elder brothers and sisters of Cecily of York, if their alliances were less exalted than hers, were yet wedded, almost without exception, to the most important members of the baronage.

Of the elder family, the offspring of Earl Ralph by Margaret of Stafford, the second son Ralph Neville of Biwell married the co-heiress of Ferrers. One sister died young, another became a nun, but four of the remaining five were married to the heirs of the houses of Mauley, Dacre, Scrope of Bolton, and Kyme. The younger family, the children of Joan of Beaufort, made even more fortunate marriages. Of the daughters, the youngest, as we have stated above, wedded Richard of York. Her elder sisters were united respectively to John Mowbray Duke of Norfolk, Humphrey Stafford Duke of Buckingham, and Henry Percy Earl of Northumberland—the grandson of Earl Ralph's old enemy and the son of Hotspur. Of the six sons of Joan of Beaufort, Richard the eldest married Alice Montacute, heiress of the earldom of Salisbury, and became by her the father of the Kingmaker; with him we shall have much to do. William, the second son, won the heiress of Fauconbridge. George, the third son, was made the heir of his half-uncle John Lord Latimer, and by special grant succeeded to his uncle's barony. Robert entered the Church, and by judicious family backing became Bishop of Salisbury before he had reached his twenty-fifth year, only to be transplanted ten years later to Durham, the most powerful of the English bishoprics, whose palatine rights he could thus turn to the use of his numerous kindred. Finally, Edward, the youngest brother, secured Elizabeth Beauchamp, heiress of Abergavenny.

The numbers of the English baronage had been rapidly decreasing since the reign of the third Edward, and in the early years of Henry the Sixth the total number of peers summoned to a Parliament never exceeded thirty-five. Among this small muster could be counted one grandson, three sons, and five sons-in-law of Earl Ralph.[2] A little later, one son and one grandson more were added to the peers of the Neville kindred, and it seemed probable that by the marriages of the next generation half the English House of Lords would be found to descend from the prolific stock of Raby.

In the first twenty years of the reign of Henry of Windsor, while the young King's personal weakness was not yet known, while his uncle of Bedford and his great-uncle of Winchester stood beside the throne, and while the war in France—though the balance had long turned against England—was still far from its disastrous end, the confederacies of the great baronial houses were of comparatively little importance. The fatal question of the succession to the Crown was still asleep, for the young King was only just nearing manhood, and might, for all that men knew, be the parent of as many war-like sons as his grandfather. It was not till Henry's nine years of barren wedlock, from 1445 to 1454, set the minds of his nobles running on the problem of the succession, that the peace of England was really endangered.

Richard Neville, the eldest of the sons of Earl Ralph's second marriage, was born in 1399. He was too young to follow King Henry to the siege of Harfleur and the fight of Agincourt, but a few years later he accompanied his half-brother John, the heir of Westmoreland, to the wars of France. It was not in France, however, that the years of his early manhood were to be spent, but on the Scotch Border in the company of his father. When he came of age and was knighted in 1420 he was made the colleague of the old Earl in the wardenship of the Western Marches. This office he retained for several years, and was in consequence much mixed up with Scotch affairs, twice acting as commissioner to treat with the Regent of Scotland, and escorting James the First to the border of his kingdom when the English Council released him from his long captivity. We hear of him occasionally at Court, as when, for example, he acted as carver at the Coronation Banquet of the newly-wed Queen Catherine, a ceremony which, according to Monstrelet, "was performed with such splendid magnificence that the like had never been seen since the time of that noble knight Arthur, King of the English and Bretons."

Richard had reached the age of twenty-six when, in 1425, he married Alice, the only child of Thomas Montacute Earl of Salisbury, who had just reached her eighteenth year. The Montacutes were not among the wealthiest of the English earls—for his faithful adherence to Richard the Second the last head of the house had lost his life and his estates; and although his son had been restored in blood, and had received back many of the Montacute lands, yet the list of his manors in the Escheats Roll reads poorly enough beside those of the Earls of Norfolk and Devon, March and Arundell. Earl Thomas, in spite of his father's fate, had consented to serve the house of Lancaster.

In 1425, as we have already mentioned, the old Earl, Ralph of Westmoreland, died. In his will, which has been preserved, we find that he left his son Richard little enough—"two chargers, twelve dishes, and a great ewer and basin of silver, a bed of Arras, with red, white, and green hangings, and four untrained horses, the best that should be found in his stable." Evidently he thought that he need do nothing for this son on whom the earldom of Salisbury was bound to devolve. It was only to Ralph and Edward, the two among his surviving sons who had not yet inherited land from their wives, that the old Earl demised the baronies of Biwell and Winlayton, two of his outlying estates.

But in another respect the will of Earl Ralph was destined to prove a source of many heart-burnings in the house of Neville, and fated to break up the strict family alliance which made its strength. While he left the Durham lands of Neville, round his ancestral castle of Raby, to his grandson and heir, Ralph the second, he made over the larger part of his Yorkshire possessions not to the young Earl, but as jointure to his widow, Joan of Beaufort, the mother of Richard and the other thirteen children of his second family. The Countess, once mistress of Sherif Hoton Castle and the other North-Riding lands of Neville, had no thought of letting them pass away from her own sons to the descendants of her husband's first wife. They were destined to be diverted from the elder to the younger family. Here lay the source of many future troubles, but while the young Earl Ralph was still a minor the matter did not come to a head.

Three years after he lost his father, Richard Neville heard of the death of his father-in-law. The Earl of Salisbury had been appointed by John of Bedford Captain-General of all the English forces in France, and gathering together ten thousand men, all that the Regent could spare, had marched to the fatal siege of Orleans. There in the early days of the leaguer, six months before Joan the Maid came to the rescue of the garrison, he had met his death. As he watched the walls from the tower on the bridge over the Loire, a stone shot had torn away half his face; he died in a few days, exhorting his officers with his last breath to persevere in the attack.

Thus Richard Neville became by the death of his father-in-law Earl of Salisbury and master of the lands of Montacute. They lay, for the most part, on the borders of Wiltshire and Hampshire, between Ringwood and Amesbury, in the valleys of the Bourn and Avon. The castles of Christchurch and Trowbridge were the most important part of the heritage from the military point of view. Some scattered manors in Berkshire, Dorset, and Somerset served to swell its value. Richard, now become a considerable South Country baron, at once did homage for his wife's lands, and was summoned as Earl of Salisbury to the next Parliament, that of 1429. At the same meeting at which he took his seat his nephew, Ralph the younger of Westmoreland, also appeared for the first time, having now passed his minority and entered into possession of such of the Neville lands as had not been left to his step-mother.

It was beyond doubt the alienation of these lands which led to the estrangement between the younger and the elder Nevilles which we soon after find taking visible form in troubles in the North. Ralph, marrying a sister of Henry Earl of Northumberland, became the firm friend and ally of that house of Percy which his grandfather had done so much to humble. Richard kept up the old feud, and was always found on the opposite side from his nephew. Presently (the exact year of the commencement of the quarrel is uncertain, but it was at its height in 1435) we find them at actual blows in a manner which brings out the fact that the "good and strong governance," which Parliament after Parliament sighed for in the reign of Henry the Sixth, had already become a hopeless dream. Plaints come down from the North to the Lord Chancellor that "owing to the grievous differences which have arisen between Ralph Earl of Westmoreland, and his brothers John and Thomas on the one hand, and Joan Dowager-Countess of Westmoreland and her son Richard Earl of Salisbury, on the other hand, have of late assembled, by manner of war and insurrection, great routs and companies upon the field, which have done all manner of great offences as well in slaughter and destruction of the King's lieges as otherwise, which things are greatly against the estate and weal and peace of this Royaume of England."

Of the details of this local war in Yorkshire we know nothing. Some sort of accommodation was patched up, by three arbitrators named by the Privy Council, for the moment between uncle and nephew; but the grudge rankled, and if ever England should be rent by civil war, it took no prophet to foretell that the two Neville earls would be found in opposite camps.

The old Countess Joan of Westmoreland died in 1440, and left, as was natural, Middleham, Sherif Hoton, and all the other lands of her jointure to her eldest son. Richard of Salisbury thus became a much greater landholder in the North than he already was in the South. His Hampshire and Wiltshire fiefs are for the future the less important centre of his strength. Sherif Hoton becomes his favourite residence, and it is always as a power in Yorkshire, not in Wessex, that he is mentioned by the chroniclers of the day.

Neither of the Neville earls took any prominent part in the never-ending French War. Ralph of Westmoreland seems to have been wanting both in the appetite for war and the keen eye for the main chance which had hitherto distinguished the lords of Raby. It was his younger brother John who was the fighting man of the older branch of Neville. Earl Richard, on the other hand, was energetic enough, but seems to have preferred to push his fortunes at home, rather than to risk his reputation in the unlucky wars where Somerset and Suffolk and so many more earned ill-fame and unpopularity. We hear of him most often on the Scottish Border, where he seems to have succeeded to the commanding position that had once been held by his father. He was Captain of Berwick, and served as Warden both of the Eastern and Western Marches, till at the end of 1435 he was sent as ambassador extraordinary to Edinburgh. James the First, with whom he had to settle some matters of Border feud, was his own connection, for Salisbury's mother was aunt of Joan Beaufort, the young Queen of Scots. After quitting King James, only a few months before his cruel murder at Perth, Earl Richard went on an embassy of far greater importance, being sent to France, along with his young brother-in-law the Duke of York, to endeavour to patch up some agreement that might end the series of disasters which had commenced with the death of the Duke of Bedford in the previous year. His mission failed, as indeed all missions were bound to do that made after the treaty of Arras the same demands which the French had refused before it. Nevertheless, on his return, in 1437, Salisbury was made a member of the Privy Council, and took his seat in the body which ever since 1422 had been directing the fortunes of England.

This appointment fixed Salisbury in London for the greater part of the next ten years. We find from the records of the Privy Council that he was almost as regular an attendant at its meetings as was Cardinal Beaufort himself, the practical Prime Minister of the realm. His signature appears at the foot of countless documents, and his activity and appetite for business seem to have been most exemplary. So far as we can judge of his action, he appears to have sided with the great Cardinal, and not with the Opposition which centred round Humphrey Duke of Gloucester; but factions had not fully developed themselves as yet in the Council, and the definite parties which existed a few years later were only just beginning to sketch themselves out.

Footnotes

1. Cecily is called Duchess of York in Earl's Ralph's will, so the children must therefore have been already married; but the consummation of the marriage was not till about 1438, when he was twenty-six and she twenty-three years of age.

2. The grandson was Ralph Earl of Westmoreland; the sons, Richard of Salisbury, William of Fauconbridge, and George of Latimer; the sons-in-law, the Dukes of York, Norfolk, and Buckingham, the Earl of Northumberland, and Lord Dacre. Later, Edward Neville Lord Abergavenny, and Roger Lord Scrope, appear; the first a son, the second a grandson.

Chapter 4

THE KINGMAKER'S YOUTH

Richard, the second child but eldest son of Richard Neville of Salisbury and Alice Montacute, was born on November 22nd, 1428, just nineteen days after his grandfather had fallen at the siege of Orleans. We know absolutely nothing of his childhood—not even the place of his birth is recorded. We must suppose, but cannot prove, that his earliest days were passed on his mother's lands in Wessex, in moving about between Amesbury, Christchurch, and Ringwood as his parents' household made its periodical peregrinations from manor to manor according to the universal practice of the time. As a boy he must have visited his paternal grandmother, Joan of Beaufort, on her Yorkshire estates, when his father was fixed in the North as Warden of the Scotch Border. There probably he may have imbibed some of the old lady's dislike for her step-sons of the elder branch of the Nevilles, with whom she and his father were now at open variance. A little later he must have spent much time in London, when his father became a member of the Council of Regency, lodged at the "Tenement called the Harbour in the Ward of Dowgate," which his father and grandmother had received by will from his grandfather when the larger London house of the family, "Neville's Inn in Silver Street," passed with the Westmoreland earldom to the elder branch.

The fortunes of the house of Neville, as we have told them hitherto, have consisted of one interminable story of fortunate marriages. The reader must now be asked to concentrate his attention on another group of these alliances, a group which settled the whole history of the Kingmaker, and gave him the title of the earldom by which he is always named.

The Beauchamps of Warwick held one of the oldest English earldoms; they represented in direct descent the Henry of Newburgh to whom William Rufus had granted the county in 1190.[3] Richard Beauchamp, the head of the family at this time, was perhaps the worthiest and the most esteemed of the English nobles of his day. The "gracious Warwick," the "father of courtesy" as the Emperor Sigismund called him, had been through all the wars of Henry the Fifth, and won therein a name only second to that of the King himself. He had seen many cities and men in every land that lay between England and Palestine, and left everywhere behind him a good report. His virtues and accomplishments had caused him to be singled out as tutor and governor to the young King, Henry the Sixth; no better model, as all agreed, could be found for the ruler of England to copy. Nor did Warwick belie his task; he made Henry upright, learned, painstaking, conscientious to a fault. If he could but have made him as strong in body and spirit as he was morally, he would have given England the best king that ever she possessed.

Richard Beauchamp had married Isabel, heiress of Despenser, and widow of Richard, Lord of Abergavenny. Their family consisted of a son, Henry, a boy of ten, and a daughter, Anne, three years younger. In addition, the Countess of Warwick had an only daughter by her first husband, who was heiress of Abergavenny. Beauchamp and Richard Neville of Salisbury were the best of friends, and had determined to seal their friendship by intermarriage between their families. The alliance was destined to be complicated; each earl married his heir to his friend's daughter. The boy Henry, heir of Warwick, was affianced to Cecily Neville, Salisbury's six-year-old daughter; the boy Richard, heir of Salisbury, to Anne Beauchamp, daughter of Warwick. Nor was this all; the family relations were complicated by the marriage of Warwick's step-daughter Elizabeth, the heiress of Abergavenny, to Edward Neville the younger brother of Salisbury.

The boy Richard Neville received a competent dowry with his wife, but nothing more was expected to follow from the marriage. Fate, however, decreed otherwise.

The old Earl of Warwick died in 1439, full of years and honours. To him succeeded his son Henry, the husband of Cecily Neville, now sixteen years of age, and "a seemly lord of person." He had been brought up with the young King, a lad of his own years, and was Henry of Lancaster's bosom friend. When the King came of age he heaped on the young Beauchamp every honour that his affection could devise. Not only was he made Knight of the Garter and a Privy Councillor before he was nineteen, but he was created Duke of Warwick, and invested by the King's own hands with the lordship of the Isle of Wight. If Henry Beauchamp had lived, it would have been he, and not Suffolk and Somerset, who in a few years would have ruled England. But his career was broken in its earliest promise. Ere he had finished his twenty-third year Henry Beauchamp was cut off from the land of the living, and his lands and duchy devolved on his only child, a little girl but four years of age. Her wardship fell to William de la Pole Earl of Suffolk, already the declared adversary of Salisbury and the Neville family.

By the wholly unexpected death of Henry Beauchamp only this one frail life lay between the lad Richard Neville—he was sixteen when his brother-in-law died—and the earldom of Warwick. Nor was that life to continue long. The child Anne Beauchamp survived for three years more, and then died, aged seven, on June 23rd, 1449. She was buried by her grandam Constance, daughter of Edmund Duke of York, before the high altar of Reading Abbey.

The heiress of Warwick was now the elder Anne, Richard Neville's young wife,[4] and in her right Richard received the Beauchamp lands from the unwilling hands of the little countess's guardian, Suffolk. The patent which created him Earl of Warwick, and joined his wife in the grant, was dated July 23rd, 1449.

Thus, in the year in which he reached his twenty-first birthday, the future Kingmaker became "Earl of Warwick, Newburgh, and Aumarle, Premier Earl of England, Baron of Elmley and Hanslape, and Lord of Glamorgan and Morgannoc." He was now a much more important personage than his own father, for the Beauchamp and Despenser manors in the West Midlands and the Welsh Marches were broader by far than the Montacute lands in Wessex, or the Neville holding round Middleham.

A short survey of the items of the Beauchamp heritage is necessary to show how wide-spread was the power which was now placed in the hands of the young Richard Neville. Perhaps the most compact block of his new possessions was the old Despenser holding in South Wales and Herefordshire, which included the castles of Cardiff, Neath, Caerphilly, Llantrussant, Seyntweonard, Ewyas Lacy, Castle-Dinas, Snodhill, Whitchurch, and Maud's Castle. Caerphilly alone was a stronghold fit to resist ten thousand men, with its tremendous rings of concentric fortification; and the massive Norman masonry of Cardiff was still ready for good service. Between Neath and Ewyas Lacy lay no less than fifty manors of the Despenser heritage. In Gloucestershire was another group of estates which the Beauchamps had got from the Despensers—of which the chief were the wide and populous manors of Tewkesbury, Sodbury, Fairford, Whittington, Chedworth, Wickwar, and Lydney. In Worcestershire there was a compact block of land along the Severn and on both its banks; the largest manors included in it were Upton-on-Severn, Hanley Castle, and Bewdley, but there were twenty-four more estates of less importance, together with the Castle of Elmley, which had given the Beauchamps a baron's title. In Warwickshire, beside the fair town and castle which went with the earldom, there were not any very broad tracts of land—only nine manors in all, but one of these was the wealthy manor of Tamworth. Going farther south in the Midlands we find in Oxfordshire five manors and the forest of Wychwood reckoned to the Beauchamps, and in Buckinghamshire the baronial seat of Hanslape and seven manors more. Nor was it only in central England that Richard Neville could count his estates; there were scattered holdings accruing to him in Kent, Hampshire, Sussex, Essex, Hertfordshire, Suffolk, Norfolk, Berkshire, Wiltshire, Somerset, Devon, Cornwall, Northampton, Stafford, Cambridge, Rutland, and Nottingham, amounting in all to forty-eight manors. Even in the distant North one isolated possession fell to him—the castle of Barnard's-Castle on the Tees. If in addition to the manors we began to count up the scattered knights' fees, the advowsons of churches, the chantries, the patronage of abbeys, and the tenements in towns, which formed part of the Beauchamp heritage, we should never be done; but these are all written in the Escheats Roll, whence the antiquary may excavate them at his will.

The year 1449, in which Richard Neville attained his majority and gathered in his wife's heritage, was the turning-point in the reign of Henry the Sixth. No more critical time could have been found in the whole century in which to place power and influence in the hands of a young, able, and ambitious man. For it was in 1449 that the doom of the house of Lancaster was settled by the final collapse of the English domination in France. In March came the fatal attack on Fougères which reopened the war, an attack of which it is hard to say whether it was more foolish or wicked. In August, September, and October occurred with bewildering rapidity the fall of the great towns of eastern and central Normandy, ending with the capitulation of Rouen after a siege of only nineteen days.

It was this unparalleled series of disasters which made the existing Lancastrian rule unbearable to the English nation. Suffolk, the minister whose policy had led up to the disaster, and Somerset, the governor whose avarice had depleted the Norman garrisons, and whose rashness and ill faith had precipitated the outbreak of hostilities, were henceforth pursued by the bitter hatred of the majority of Englishmen. When it was found that King Henry identified their cause with his own, he himself—against whom no one had previously breathed a word—found for the first time that the current of public opinion was setting against him.

It was now that the final scission of the two parties that were afterwards to be known as Yorkist and Lancastrian took place. Every man of note in England had now to make his choice whether his personal loyalty to the King should lead him into acquiescing in the continuance in office of the ministers whom Henry openly favoured, or whether he would set himself in opposition to the Court faction, even though he was thereby led into opposition to the King.

From the first moment there was no doubt which of the two courses would be adopted by the two Neville earls of the younger branch. Warwick, now as always, acted in strict union with his father, and Salisbury had never been a friend of Suffolk. Moreover, they were both concerned in behalf of their relative the Duke of York, who by Somerset's contrivance had been sent into a kind of honorary exile in Ireland. When the crisis should come, it was already pretty certain that Salisbury and Warwick would be found on the side of York, and not on that of Suffolk and Somerset. But as yet, though men were growing excited and preparing for evil times, no one foresaw the exact shape which the troubles were to take. One thing only was certain, that Suffolk and Somerset were growing so hateful to the nation that an explosion against them would soon take place, and that when the explosion came there would be a large party among the leading men of England who would rejoice in its effects.

The most ominous sign of the times was that the great barons on both sides were already quietly arming, seeing to the numbers of their retainers, and concluding agreements to take their neighbours into their livery if the worst should come to the worst.

Nothing can be a more typical sign of the times than the treaty which Salisbury entered into with a Westmoreland knight, whose lands lay not far from his great holding in the North-Riding, as early as September 1449, the very month when Somerset was losing Normandy.

"This indenture made between Richard Earl of Salisbury, on the one part, and Walter Strykelande knight, on the other, beareth witness that the said Walter is retained and withholded with the said Earl for the term of his life, against all folk, saving his allegiance to the King. And the said Walter shall be well and conveniently horsed, armed, and arrayed, and always ready to bide come and go with to and for the said Earl, at all times and places, as well in time of peace as time of war, at the wages of the same Earl." Walter's following was worth having, being "servants, tenants, and inhabitants within the county of Westmoreland; bowmen with horse and harness, sixty-nine; billmen horsed and harnessed, seventy-four; bowmen without horses, seventy-one; billmen without horses, seventy-six"—in fact a little army of two hundred and ninety men. The existence of a few such treaties as this between Salisbury and his northern neighbours shows clearly enough how the Neville power was built up, and how formidable to the public peace it might become. If once such treaties were in existence, how long would it be before the single clause "saving his allegiance" would begin to drop into oblivion?

Footnotes

<u>3</u>. The Beauchamps came into the title in 1268, William de Beauchamp having married the grand-daughter of Henry of Newburgh, whose male issue had died out.

<u>4</u>. Anne was the only heir of the full blood to Henry Duke of Warwick, but he had several half-sisters, to whom the reversion of the title was left by the patent which gave Richard and Anne Neville the earldom.

Charles W. Oman

Chapter 5

THE CAUSE OF YORK

If 1449, the year of Warwick's accession to his wife's heritage, was a time of trouble for England, the year which immediately followed was far worse. The loss of the Norman fortresses was followed in a few months by the sporadic outbreaks of popular rage which might have been expected—outbreaks directed against all who could in any way be connected with the evil governance of the realm. Bishop Moleyns, the Keeper of the Privy Seal, was murdered by a mob of mutinous sailors at Portsmouth in January. But this blow was only a premonitory symptom of the storm which was brewing against Suffolk, the head of the Government. Four months later—the fatal battle of Formigny had been fought meanwhile, and the last English foothold in Northern France lost—he was driven from power by an irresistible demonstration of wrath, in which the whole nation, from the House of Lords to the London mob, took its part. Protected from legal punishment by the King's pardon, Suffolk fled over-sea; but some London ships waylaid him in the Straits of Dover, and he was seized and put to death after a mock trial by the captain of the Nicholas of the Tower. So well hated was he that his tragic end was received with exultation instead of remorse, and the political ballad-mongers of the day wrote many an insulting rhyme over his headless corpse.

Instead of mending matters, Suffolk's death was only the signal for worse troubles. Two months after his death came the great rebellion of the Kentishmen under Cade, accompanied by various other outbreaks in the southern counties. The insurgents were inspired by the same impulse which had slain Suffolk; they were set on making an end of all who had been responsible for the late disaster abroad and misgovernment at home. In London, Lord Say the Treasurer was caught and slain; in Wiltshire, Bishop Ayscough was beheaded by a mob of his own tenantry. But the rising, being but a sudden ebullition of rage with no plan or programme of reform, and being headed not by any respectable leader but merely by the disreputable adventurer Cade, died down of its own accord, without leaving any permanent effect on the governance of the realm. To make its power felt, the national discontent had to look for a responsible leader and a definite programme.

Both the Court party and the people knew where that leader might be found. Richard Duke of York, the heir-apparent to the childless King, lay across the sea in Ireland. He was an able soldier, much tried in the French wars, a firm and successful administrator—he had even succeeded in winning popularity in Ireland—and a man of blameless character, who had completely won the nation's confidence. Moreover, he was a man with a grievance; though the first prince of the blood, he was deliberately excluded from all place in the King's councils or share in the administration of the realm. While in the midst of a successful campaign in France he had been superseded by the unlucky Somerset, and sent off to Ireland, apparently in the idea that like most other rulers of that distressful country he would wreck his reputation there. But he had been fortunate, and only increased his fame by the administration of the island. Already the Court party were murmuring against him once more, and the people believed that some other exile would ere long be found for him. As the ballad-monger sang—

The falcon flies and has no rest

 Till he wot where he may build his nest.

Cade's rebels had used the Duke's name largely in their proclamations, but there seems no real ground for supposing that they had held any communication with him. The only evidence against him was that all discontented parties and persons spoke of him as the man that should right them some day. Nevertheless threats were made that he should be indicted for high treason, and action against him was apparently imminent. Then at last York took the initiative. He threw up the government of Ireland, crossed over to Wales, and came up to London with a considerable body of his tenants from the Marches at his back. There he claimed and obtained an interview with the King, in which he declared his loyalty, and received Henry's assurance that no harm was intended against him. This done, he retired to his estates on the Welsh border. But he had now definitely put himself at the head of the opposition to the Court party, whom he had bitterly rated in his remonstrance to the King.

The discontent of England had found its mouthpiece and its leader in this resolute prince, "a man of low stature, with a short square face, and somewhat stout of body," like his uncle Edmund of York, who had fallen at Agincourt rather stifled in his armour than slain by his wounds.

Our whole view of the conduct of Warwick in the ten years between 1450 and 1460 must be determined by our decision as to the designs and conduct of his uncle of York during that period. If we conclude that the Duke was aiming at the crown from the first, then we cannot but believe that his brother-in-law Salisbury and his nephew Warwick must have known or guessed his wishes, and on them must rest almost as great a share of blame for the outbreak of the Civil War as lies on the head of York himself. For the gain of their family we must believe that they sacrificed the peace of their country. This view has been commonly adopted by historians; it was set forth in every Lancastrian manifesto of the time; it was repeated by the historians who wrote under the Tudors, and it still prevails.

Another view, however, was taken by the majority of the English people in York's own day. Wherever in England public spirit ran strong, wherever wealth had accumulated and civilisation had advanced, a sympathy for the Yorkist party manifested itself. Kent, London, and East Anglia were always strongly on the Duke's side. But if York had been an ambitious schemer, deliberately upsetting the peace of the realm for his own ends, we should not expect to find his supporters among those parts of the nation to whom peace and good governance were above all things profitable.

A glance through the pages of the chroniclers who were contemporary with the war, Harding, Gregory, William of Worcester, Whethamsted, the anonymous English chronicler in the Camden Series, shows that to the majority of the English people York passed not as a disturber of the peace, but as a wronged and injured man, goaded into resistance by the machinations of the Court party. In one aspect he was regarded as a great lord of the royal blood excluded from his rightful place at the Council board, and even kept out of the country by his enemies who had the

King's ear. In another he was regarded as the leader and mouthpiece of the Opposition of the day, of the old and popular war-party which inherited the traditions of Henry the Fifth and Humphrey of Gloucester—a party, indeed, whose views (as we have said elsewhere) were unwise and even immoral, but one which might reasonably ask to be taken into consideration by those who managed the affairs of the realm. In these days of ours when Ministries prove incapable and grow discredited the Opposition has its turn at the helm in the natural course of things. In the fifteenth century the old methods which had served Simon de Montfort, and the Lords Ordainers of 1322, were still the only ones which could be used against ministers who were out of sympathy with the nation. York was doing at St. Albans much what Earl Simon had done at Lewes.

This too must be said, that if disaster without and disorder within are to be held sufficient to discredit any rule, there had never been a time since the evil days of Bannockburn when England had more right to be discontented with her rulers. Moreover, there was no chance that things would grow better; as long as the Queen and her friends ruled the King, so long would things continue as they were. Men thought at one moment that with the removal of Suffolk the evil times would come to an end. But when an outburst of popular fury swept Suffolk to his end—and be it remembered that there is no evidence to connect York with Suffolk's tragic death—the ascendency of Somerset proved as disastrous and as hopeless as that of his predecessor. And when Somerset fell at St. Albans men hoped once more that matters would right themselves; but the less-known ministers who soon succeeded to the helm—Beaumont and the Earl of Wiltshire—proved quite as unprofitable servants to the nation. As long as the Queen was at the King's side to choose his councillors for him, so long would the discontent of England continue to increase. Margaret's misfortunes make us loath to speak evil of her, but in fairness to the Yorkists it must be remembered that she was the most detestable politician that England had known. It is usual to call the dislike of the nation for her a stupid prejudice against a foreigner; but there was surely some reason for hating the woman who sold Berwick to the Scots and Calais to the French, who reintroduced the hateful practice of sweeping attainders in the Parliament of 1459, who succeeded in turning loyalty into a party-cry by making the King a party-leader. Well might she confess to a foreign friend on one occasion "that if the great lords of her own party knew what she was doing, they would themselves be the first to rise and put her to death," for she it was who committed that foulest treason of all—which consists in sending secretly to tell a foreign enemy where to strike, in order that by his blow a party-end may be served. In 1457, when the realm was for a moment at peace, she deliberately incited the French admirals to make their great descent on the Kentish coast which ended in the fearful sack of Sandwich, merely because she knew that such a disaster would be counted against her political enemies the Yorkists. There is nothing to be compared to it in English history except the conduct of the arch-traitor Marlborough in 1694 over the affair of Brest.

The English hatred of Queen Margaret was no prejudice, but a wholesome instinct which led the English nation to recognise its enemy. She made herself a party-leader, and as a party-leader she had to be treated. York's ten years' strife with her must be regarded not so much as the rebellion of a subject against his sovereign, but as the struggle of one party-leader against another with the primitive weapons which alone were possible in the constitutional crises of that day. But even if we grant that York had his excuses, and that his general attitude does not stand self-condemned at the first glance, it remains to be seen how far his programme was justifiable, and how far he honestly endeavoured to carry it out to the best of his abilities. That he was an able, self-confident, ambitious man, with the fixed idea that he was the victim of the intrigues of the Court party, and that but for those intrigues he would be able to assume the position in the King's Council to which his birth entitled him, we know well. That when the King remained childless for nine years after his marriage, York could not help dwelling on the near prospect of his accession to the throne, was matter of notoriety. When that prospect was suddenly taken from him by the unexpected birth of an heir to the crown, York's spirits were deeply dashed, and his friends murmured in secret about changelings and bastards. But his own attitude and language were still everything that could be required by the most exacting critic; he shared in the rejoicings at the birth of Prince Edward, and joined the Commission which was appointed to confer on the infant the title of Prince of Wales. All his speeches and manifestoes for the next six years were full even to satiety of professions of loyalty to the King, and no claims on his own part were ever made for anything more than that right of access to the King's ear to which he was obviously entitled. The Yorkist declarations are always statements of grievance and demands for reform, set forth on public grounds; they show no traces of dynastic claims. The actions of the party, too, are quite in keeping with their declarations. That they would take the King into their own hands, and not leave him in those of the Somersets or Wiltshire or Beaumont, they had always stated, and they attempted no more when they had the chance. The best criterion of York's honesty is his conduct after the first battle of St. Albans, when the fortune of war had placed the King's person in his power. He then proceeded to give Henry new ministers, but did absolutely nothing more. No word about the succession was breathed, nor was it even attempted to punish those who had previously ruled the kingdom so ill. With a wise moderation all the blame was heaped on Somerset—and Somerset was dead, and could suffer no harm whatever might be laid to his charge.

It may then fairly be argued that Warwick and all those who followed Richard of York in peace and war down to the year 1460 had an honest programme, and could in all sincerity trust their leader, when he assured them that his ends were national and not personal,—the reform of the governance of England, not the establishment of the house of York on the throne. We shall see that when, after enduring and inflicting many evils, York did at last lay claim to the throne, his own party, headed by Warwick, firmly withstood him and compelled him, in adherence to his and their original pledges, to leave King Henry his throne and content himself with the prospect of an ultimate succession.

This being so, it is only just to Warwick and the other Yorkist leaders to give them the benefit of the doubt wherever their conduct admits of an honourable explanation, and not to judge their earlier assertions or claims or complaints in the light of later events. On these lines we shall proceed to describe the young Earl's actions down to the final outbreak of war in 1459.

Chapter 6

THE BEGINNING OF THE CIVIL WAR: ST ALBANS

From the moment when York returned from Ireland without the King's permission, and commenced to expostulate with his royal kinsman against the doings of Somerset and the rest of the Court party, the progress of events was sure and steady. Nothing save some extraordinary chance could have warded off the inevitable Civil War. That it did not break out sooner was only due to the fact that York was as cautious as he was determined, and was content to wait for the crown which the King's sickly constitution and long-barren wedlock promised him. Moreover, the Court party themselves had no desire to push matters to extremities against the man who was in all probability to become their king at no very distant date. For more than four years the struggle between York and Somerset proceeded before swords were actually drawn; they fought by manifestoes and proclamations, by Acts of Parliament, by armed demonstrations, but neither would actually strike the first blow.

The final crisis was brought about by the juxtaposition of two events of very different character. In August 1453 the King fell into a melancholy madness, exactly similar to that which had afflicted his unfortunate grandfather Charles the Sixth of France. He sat for days without moving or speaking; whatever was said to him he cast down his eyes and answered nought. The King's insanity was a deadly blow to Somerset, for he was helpless without the royal name to back him. York, on the other hand, with the general consent of the nation, assumed the direction of affairs, and became the King's lieutenant. He was afterwards made Protector of the Realm. This promised a final termination to the civil troubles of the realm.

But a few months after the King had become deranged, the whole face of affairs was changed by the birth of an heir to the crown. The Queen was delivered of a son on October 13th. This unexpected event—for the royal pair had been childless for nine years—was of fatal import to York. It took away the safety that had proceeded from the fact that his enemies believed that he was one day to reign over them, and it made York himself desperate. He came to the conclusion that he must be either regent or nothing; to save his head he must resort to desperate measures, and no more shrink from arms.

It is at this moment that Warwick begins to come to the front. In the earlier phases of York's struggle with Somerset he and his father had avoided committing themselves unreservedly to their kinsman's party; when he made his armed demonstration in 1452 they had not appeared at his side, but had negotiated in his favour with the King. In the Parliament of January 1454 they took part more decidedly in his favour. Mischief was brewing and every peer came up to London with hundreds of retainers in his train. It was then noticed that Warwick "with a goodly fellowship at his back" rode up in company with his uncle of York, and that Salisbury with seven score men-at-arms joined him in London.

York's preponderance in the councils of the realm was at once followed by the promotion of his Neville kinsmen. In December Warwick, now aged twenty-five, was made a member of the Privy

Council. In April, after York had been made Protector, Salisbury was made Chancellor of the Realm; it was forty-four years since a layman had held the post.

The King was insane for sixteen months, and for that time York governed the realm with discretion and success. His conduct with regard to the question of the succession was scrupulously correct. The infant Prince Edward was acknowledged heir to the throne, and York, Warwick, and Salisbury were all members of the Commission which in April invested him with the title of Prince of Wales. The Court party were treated with leniency; only Somerset, against whom the popular outcry was as loud as ever (he had nearly been torn to pieces by a London mob in 1453), was committed to custody in the Tower, where he lay all the time of the King's madness. The country seemed satisfied and the prospect was fair.

To the Nevilles these two last years of promotion and success had only been clouded by a fierce quarrel with the house of Percy. In 1453 Salisbury had been celebrating the marriage of his fourth son, Thomas, to a niece of Lord Cromwell at Tattershall in Yorkshire. As he left the feast his retainers fell into an affray with some followers of Thomas Percy Lord Egremont, a younger son of the Earl of Northumberland. Out of this small spark sprung a sudden outbreak of private war all over the counties of York and Northumberland, in which the Nevilles were headed by John, Salisbury's second son, and the Percies by Egremont. The trouble lasted more than a year, and was only ended by York going in person, after he had been made Protector, to pacify the combatants. In this he succeeded, but the Percies maintained that they had been wronged, and were ever afterwards strong supporters of Somerset and the Queen.

In December 1454 King Henry came to his senses, and York resigned the protectorate. The King's recovery was in every way unfortunate; the moment that he was himself again he fell back into the hands of the Court party. His first act was to release Somerset from the Tower, and declare him a true and faithful subject. His next was to dismiss York and Salisbury from all their offices, and with them several other high functionaries who were enemies of Somerset, including Tiptoft Earl of Worcester, the Lord Treasurer. The disgraced peers retired to their estates—York to Sendal, Salisbury to Middleham.

But worse was to come. In May a Council, to which were summoned neither York, Salisbury, Warwick, nor any other of the old councillors who were their friends, met at Westminster. This body summoned a Parliament to meet at Leicester, "for the purpose of providing for the safety of the King's person against his enemies." Who would be declared the enemies York and Salisbury could guess without difficulty; and what would be done with these enemies they knew well enough. Imprisonment would be the least evil to be feared at the hands of Somerset.

The fatal moment had come. York was desperate, and resolved to anticipate the vengeance of his adversaries. The moment that the news came, he called out his Yorkshire retainers, and sent to ask the aid of his friends all over England. Salisbury joined him at once with the Neville tenants from his North-Riding estates, and without a moment's delay York and his brother-in-law marched on London. Warwick fell in with them on the way, but no other friend came to their aid, though the Duke of Norfolk was getting together a considerable force on their behalf in East Anglia.

York's little army marched down the Ermine Street; on May 20th he lay at Royston in Cambridgeshire. Beside the two Nevilles he had only one other peer in his company, Lord Clinton, and the knights present were merely the personal followers of York and Salisbury. Except a few of Warwick's Midland tenants, the whole army was composed of the Yorkshire retainers of York and Salisbury, and the chroniclers speak of the whole army as the Northern Men. More troops could have been had by waiting, but the Duke knew that if he delayed, the enemy would also gain time to muster in strength. At present the lords of the King's Council were quite unprepared for war, and the rapid march of York's little army had not allowed them time for preparation.

On the 21st the Duke felt his way southward along the line of the Ermine Street, and lay at Ware. There he and the two Earls indited a laborious apology for their arrival in arms to "their most redoubted sovereign Lord the King." They were "coming in grace, as true and humble liegemen, to declare and show at large their loyalty," and sought instant admission to the royal presence that they might convince him of the "sinister, malicious, and fraudulent reports of their enemies."

Somerset read clearly enough the meaning of York's march on London, and even before the Duke's manifesto was received, had stirred up the King to have recourse to arms. Many of the great lords of the King's party were in London, but they were surprised by the sudden approach of the enemy, and had brought few followers with them. Thus it came to pass that although the King marched out of Westminster on the 21st with many of the greatest lords of England at his back, he had less than three thousand combatants in his host. With him went forth his half-brother Jasper of Pembroke, the Dukes of Somerset and Buckingham, the Earls of Northumberland, Devon, Stafford, Wiltshire, and Dorset, and Lords Clifford, Dudley, Berners, and Roos, nearly a quarter of the scanty peerage of England. York's manifesto reached the King as he marched through Kilburn, but Somerset sent it back without allowing it to reach the royal hands. That night the army turned off the Roman road to shelter themselves in the houses of Watford; but next morning very early all were afoot again, and long before seven o'clock King Henry and his host reached St. Albans. The royal banner was pitched in St. Peter's Street, at the northern end of the straggling little town, the outlets of the streets were barricaded, and then the troops dispersed to water their horses and prepare breakfast. An hour later York and his forces appeared, advancing cautiously from the east along the Hertford Road. Hearing of the King's march on Watford, the Duke had left the direct line of advance on London, and set out to seek his enemies. When St. Albans was found to be strongly held, York, Salisbury, and Warwick drew up their four thousand men in battle array, in a field called Keyfield to the east of the town, and paused before attacking. They were hardly arrived before the Duke of Buckingham was seen emerging with a herald from the barricade which closed the eastern outlet of the town. This elderly nobleman was Salisbury's brother-in-law and Warwick's uncle; he was sure of a fair hearing from the insurgents, for he had never been identified with the party of Suffolk and Somerset, and was in arms out of pure loyalty to the King. Arrived in the presence of the rebel leaders, Humphrey of Buckingham demanded the cause of their coming and the nature of their intentions. The Duke of York replied by charging his master's envoy with a message for the royal ears, which began with all manner of earnest protestations of loyalty, proceeded with a vague declaration that the intent of his coming in arms was righteous and true, and ended with a peremptory demand that it would please the King "to deliver up such persons as he might accuse, to be dealt with like as they have deserved." Buckingham brought the message back and repeated it to the King, as he sat in the house of Westley, the Hundredman of the town of St. Albans, whither he had retired after his arrival. When the Duke's demand was made known, for once in his life the saintly King burst out into a fit of passion. "Now I shall know," he cried, "what traitors are so bold as to raise a host against me in my own land. And by the faith that I owe to St. Edward and the Crown of England, I will destroy them every mother's son, to have example to all traitors who make such rising of people against their King and Governour. And for a conclusion, say that rather than they shall have any lord here with me at this time, I will this day for his sake and in this quarrel stand myself to live or die."

When this answer came to the Duke of York he made no immediate attack on the town, but turned to harangue his troops. He told them that the King refused all reformation or reparation, that the fate of England lay in their hands, and that at the worst an honourable death in the field was better than the shame of a traitor's end, which awaited them if they lost the day. Then he launched the whole body in three divisions against the barricades which obstructed the northern, southern, and eastern exits of the town.

The hour was half-past eleven o'clock, for the interchange of messages between the King and York had consumed four hours of the morning. The royal troops, seeing Buckingham coming and going between the two armies, had believed that an agreement would be patched up without fighting. Many had left their posts, and some had disarmed themselves. When the Duke's men were seen in motion every man ran to arms, and the bells of the abbey and the churches ringing the alarm set monks and townsmen to prayers, in good hope that the shield of their warrior-patron would be stretched over them to ward off the plundering bands from the North, the

> Gens Boreæ, gens perfidiæ, gens prona rapinæ,

whose advent always sent Abbot Whethamsted into an ecstasy of bad Latin verses.

The first rush of the Yorkists was beaten off at all the three points which they attacked. Lord Clifford on the London Road "kept the barriers so strongly that the Duke might not in any wise, for all the power he had, break into the streets." Warwick too, who led the left division of the Yorkist host, was repulsed in his attack on the southern exit of the town. But the Earl's quick military eye, now for the first time exercised, had marked that the Lancastrians, though strong enough to hold the barricades, had not enough men to defend the long straggling line of houses which formed the southern extension of the town. Gathering together his repulsed retainers, he broke into the gardens which lay behind the houses of Holywell Street, and bursting open the back-doors of several dwellings, ran out into the main thoroughfare of the town, "between the sign of the Chequers and the sign of the Key, blowing up his trumpets and shouting with a great voice, A Warwick! A Warwick!"—a cry destined to strike terror into Lancastrian ears on many a future battlefield. Warwick's sudden irruption took the defenders of the barricades in the rear, but they faced about and stood to it manfully in the streets. The Lancastrian line was broken, and the Yorkist centre, where Sir Robert Ogle led on the Duke's own followers from the Northern Marches, now burst into the market-place in the centre of the town to aid Warwick.

For one wild half-hour the arrows flew like sleet up and down St. Peter's Street, and the knights fought hand to hand in the narrow roadway. But the Lancastrians were overmatched. The King received an arrow in the neck, and was led bleeding into the house of a tanner. Somerset, the cause of the battle, was stricken dead on the doorstep of an inn named the Castle. Sir Philip Wentworth, the King's standard-bearer, threw down his banner and fled away. James of Ormond the Irish Earl of Wiltshire, and Thorpe the Speaker of the House of Commons, followed him. But the other leaders of the King's army were less fortunate. The Earl of Northumberland and Lord Clifford were slain. The Earl of Dorset was desperately wounded, and left for dead in the street. The Duke of Buckingham, with an arrow sticking in his face, took sanctuary in the abbey. The Earls of Stafford and Devon, both wounded, and

Lord Dudley, yielded themselves prisoners. Only six score men had been slain in the King's army, but the larger part were persons of mark, for, as was often the case in that century, the lightly-equipped archers and billmen could fling down their arms and get away with ease, while the knights and nobles, fighting on foot in their cumbrous armour, could not make speed to fly when the day was lost. So it came to pass that of the one hundred and twenty Lancastrians who fell, only forty-eight were common men, the rest were nobles, knights, and squires, or officers of the King's household. On the next day the victors marched on London, vainly hoping, perhaps, that with the death of Somerset and the capture of the King the days of the weak government of Lancaster were over.

The Duke and his followers thought, as yet, of nothing more than a change of ministry. Their conduct shows that they had nothing more in hand than the replacing of the Court party in the great offices of State by persons who should be more in touch with their own views and the will of the nation. The Chancellorship was left in the hands of Archbishop Bourchier, whom the Yorkists felt that they could trust; but the Earl of Wiltshire was replaced as Treasurer by Lord Bourchier, the Archbishop's brother. The Duke of York became Constable; Warwick superseded the dead Somerset as Captain of Calais; Salisbury was made Steward of the Duchy of Lancaster. A little later Warwick's younger brother George Neville was given the wealthy bishopric of Exeter, though he had only just reached his twenty-sixth year. A Parliament summoned in July ratified these appointments, and chose as its Speaker Sir John Wenlock, of whom we shall frequently hear again as one of Warwick's firmest friends and adherents. A strongly-worded oath of allegiance to King Henry was taken by the Duke of York, and all the House of Lords with him, and the new ministry started on its career with favourable prospects. The only trouble for the moment came from an ill-judged attempt in Parliament to fix the responsibility for the "Ill Day of St. Albans" on definite persons. Warwick named Lord Cromwell as one of those most to blame, and when Cromwell gave an angry reply, there sprang up such an altercation between them that men feared a breach of the peace. That night Cromwell borrowed the Earl of Shrewsbury's men-at-arms to guard his house; but Warwick had cooled down and no more came of the quarrel, for the Parliament very wisely concluded to lay all the responsibility for the Civil War on Somerset, who was dead and could not reply.

York's authority in the kingdom was made more secure for the moment when King Henry fell once again into one of his fits of melancholy madness in October. The Parliament reassembled and appointed the Duke Regent, but on February 25th Henry came to his senses, and at once relieved York of his office. There followed a time of unrest and rumours of war, but for some months longer the Duke succeeded in maintaining his place at the helm. But trouble was always impending. Warwick, whose trained and paid soldiery in the garrison of Calais were the only permanent military force belonging to the Crown, had to come over on several occasions to back his uncle. At one time we hear that York feared to be waylaid on his way to Parliament, and got Warwick with three hundred men "all in jacks or brigandines" to escort him thither, "saying that if he had not come so strong he would have been distressed, but no man knew by whom, for men think verily that there is no man able to undertake any such enterprise."

York was not wrong, however, in thinking that there were those who were ready to risk much to get him out of power. Since Somerset was dead, the leadership of the Court party had fallen into very firm and determined hands, those of Margaret of Anjou, and the Queen had resolved to exercise the unbounded influence that she enjoyed over her husband to make him evict his Yorkist ministers the moment that it seemed safe so to do. For her resolve she had this much excuse, that the new government was at first no more fortunate than the old in enforcing order in the kingdom, for into the period of York's ascendency fell the worst private war that had been seen for a generation. Courtney Earl of Devon and Lord Bonville fell to blows in the West, and fought a battle outside Exeter with four thousand men a side; the Earl won, and signalised his victory by ransacking the cathedral and carrying off several of the canons as prisoners. Yet he was not brought to justice for this abominable sacrilege, even though he was of the party which was opposed to York. But Margaret was not entitled to blame York for the state of the kingdom, for we find that she deliberately went to work to give the Duke trouble, by stirring up foreign enemies against England. A Scotch raid in the summer of 1456 was more than suspected to be due to her intrigues; and it is certain that while the Duke was officially taking the Scots to task in the King's name, the King was disavowing York's war-like despatches in private letters to James the Second. When we know that a year later Margaret was not above setting on the French to ravage the Kentish sea-ports for her own private purposes, we can understand a little of the hatred with which she was followed by the Commons of the south-eastern counties.

Charles W. Oman

Chapter 7

WARWICK CAPTAIN OF CALAIS AND ADMIRAL

It was in the four years which lay between the fight of St. Albans and the second outbreak of the Civil War in 1459 that Warwick made his reputation and won his popularity. Up to 1455 he had been known merely as a capable young nobleman who followed in all things the lead of his father Salisbury. He had not as yet been given any independent command, nor trusted alone in any business of importance, though he was already far beyond the age at which many personages of the fifteenth century began to take a prominent part in politics. He was now twenty-seven years old, eleven years older than Henry the Fifth when he took over the government of Wales, nine years older than Edward the Fourth when he won the fight of Mortimer's Cross. There were no signs in Warwick of that premature development which made so many of his contemporaries grown men at sixteen, and worn-out veterans at forty.

Unlike most of his house, Warwick had not been blessed with a large family. Anne Beauchamp had borne him two daughters only, both of them delicate girls who did not live to see their thirtieth year. No male offspring was ever granted him, and it seemed evident that the lands of Warwick and Despenser were destined to pass once more into the female line. But the day was far distant when this was to be, and Richard Neville's sturdy frame and constitution,—his altitudo animi cum paribus corporis viribus, to quote Polidore Vergil,—promised many a long year of vigorous manhood.

Warwick had already become a prominent figure in English politics, not so much from the breadth of his lands or from the promise of military prowess that he had shown at St. Albans, as from the almost universal popularity which he enjoyed. He was far from being the haughty noble, the Last of the Barons, whom later writers have drawn for us. His contemporaries speak of him rather as the idol of the Commons and the people's friend: "his words were gentle, and he was affable and familiar with all men, and never spoke of his own advancement, but always of the augmentation and good governance of the realm." There never was any peer who was a better lord to his own retainers, nor was there any who bore himself more kindly towards the Commons; hence he won a personal popularity to which his father Salisbury never attained, and which even his uncle of York could not rival.

As a school for a man of action there could have been no better post than the governorship of Calais. The place had been beset by the French ever since the loss of Normandy in 1450, and was never out of danger of a sudden attack. Three times in the last six years considerable armies had marched against it, and had only been turned away by unexpected events in other quarters. Bickering with the French garrisons of Boulogne and other neighbouring places never ended, even in times of nominal truce. To cope with the enemy the Captain of Calais had a garrison always insufficient in numbers, and generally in a state of suppressed mutiny; for one of the chief symptoms of the evil rule of Suffolk and Somerset had been the impotence of the central government to find money for the regular war-expenses of the realm. The garrison of Calais was perpetually in arrears of pay, and successive governors are found complaining again and again that they were obliged to empty their own pockets to keep the soldiers to their post. Even the town-walls had been allowed to fall into disrepair for want of money to mend them.

Besides his military duties the Captain of Calais had other difficult functions. He lay on the frontier of Flanders, and a great part of the trade between England and the dominions of the house of Burgundy passed through his town, for Calais was the "staple" for that branch of commerce. Hence he had to keep on good terms with the neighbouring Burgundian governors, and also—what was far more difficult—to endeavour to sweep the Straits of Dover clear of pirates and of French privateers, whenever there was not an English fleet at sea. This was no sinecure, for of late English fleets had been rarely seen, and when they did appear had gone home without effecting anything useful. The man who could with a light heart undertake to assume the post of Captain of Calais must have been both able and self-confident.

Warwick held the place from August 1455 to August 1460, and combined with it the post of "Captain to guard the Sea" from October 1457 to September 1459. His tenure of office was in every way successful. The garrison was brought up to its full strength, and put in good discipline—largely, we may suspect, at the expense of the Earl's own pocket, for after October 1456, when the Duke of York ceased to be Protector, Warwick got little money or encouragement from England. He raised the strength of his troops to about two thousand men, and was then able to assume the offensive against the neighbouring French garrisons. His greatest success was when, in the spring of the third year of his office, he led a body of eight hundred combatants on a daring raid as far as Étaples, forty miles down the coast of Picardy, and took the town together with a fleet of wine-ships from the south of France, which he put up to ransom, and so raised a sum large enough to pay his men for some months. Falling into a disagreement also with the Burgundian governors in Flanders, he made such havoc in the direction of Gravelines and St. Omer that Duke Philip was obliged to strengthen his garrisons there, and finally was glad to consent to a pacification. The negotiations were held in Calais and came to a successful conclusion, for a commercial treaty was concluded with Flanders as well as a mere suspension of arms.

While Warwick lay at Calais he could not pay very frequent visits to England, for French alarms were always abounding. In June 1456, for example, "men said that the siege should come to Calais, for much people had crossed the water of Somme, and great navies were on the sea." Again, in May 1457, another threatened attack caused the Earl to lay in great stores, for which he had to draw on Kent: "so he had the folks of Canterbury and Sandwich before him, and thanked them for their good hearts in victualling of Calais, and prayed them for continuance therein." That those rumours of coming trouble were not all vain was shown a few months later, for a Norman fleet under Peter de Brézé threw four thousand men ashore near Sandwich in August, and the French stormed the town from the land side, held it for a day, and sacked it from garret to cellar. It was this disaster which England owed to Margaret of Anjou, for she had deliberately suggested the time and place of attack to de Brézé, in order to bring discredit on the government of the Duke of York.

It is curious to note how the work of the day of St. Albans was undone, without any violent shock, during the earlier years of Warwick's rule at Calais. The Queen played her game more cautiously than usual. First, York's protectorate was ended, on the excuse that the King, whose mind had failed him again after St. Albans, was now himself once more. Then, eight months later, a great Council was summoned, not at London, where York was too popular, but at Coventry. The meeting was packed with the men-at-arms of the Queen's adherents, and at it King Henry dismissed the two Bourchier brothers, York's firm supporters, from their offices of Chancellor and Treasurer, and replaced them by the Earl of Shrewsbury, a strong adherent of the Court party, and by Wainfleet Bishop of Winchester. It was widely believed that York, who had come to the Council with no knowledge of the Queen's intended coup d'état, would have met with an ill end if his kinsman the Duke of Buckingham had not succeeded in aiding him to escape. Of all the offices bestowed as the result of St. Albans fight, Warwick's post at Calais was the only one which was not now forfeited. Probably the Queen and her friends preferred to keep him over-sea as much as possible.

It is a good testimony to the loyalty of the Duke and his friends that they made no stir on their eviction from office. York retired to Wigmore, and for the next year abode quietly upon his estates. Salisbury went to Middleham and remained in the North. Meanwhile the country showed its discontent with the renewed rule of the Queen. Tumultuous gatherings took place in

Oxfordshire and Berkshire, and again on the Welsh Border, although no leading Yorkist was implicated in them. The temper of London was so discontented that the Queen would not allow the King to approach it for a whole year.

The ascendency of the Earls of Wiltshire, Beaumont, Shrewsbury, Exeter, and the other lords who ruled in the King's name and by the Queen's guidance, proved as unfortunate and as unpopular as any of the other periods during which Margaret's friends were at the helm. Men felt that civil war was destined to break out once more, as soon as York should be pressed too hard and find his patience at an end. Hence general joy was felt when in January 1458 the King, taking the initiative for once, announced that he was about to reconcile all the private grievances of his lords, and invited York, Salisbury, and Warwick, with the rest of their party, to attend a great Council at Westminster. They came, but fearing some snare of the Queen's, came with a numerous following—York with a hundred and forty horse, Salisbury with four hundred, Warwick with six hundred men of the Calais garrison all apparelled in red jackets emblazoned with the Beauchamp badge of the ragged staff. There was no snare in the King's invitation, and all precautions were taken to prevent affrays. The Yorkist lords and their retainers were lodged within the city, while the Queen's friends, who appeared in great force—the Earl of Northumberland alone brought three thousand men—were provided for in the suburbs. The Mayor of London—Godfrey Bulleyn, Anne Bulleyn's ancestor—with five thousand citizens arrayed in arms kept the streets, to guard against brawling between the retainers of the two parties.

The King at once set forth his purpose of a general pacification, and found York and his friends very ready to fall in with his views. More trouble was required to induce the sons of those who had fallen at St. Albans—the young Somerset, Clifford, and Northumberland—to pardon those on whose swords was their fathers' blood. But the King's untiring efforts produced the desired result. York, Salisbury, and Warwick promised to endow the Abbey of St. Albans with a sum of £45 a year, to be spent in masses for the souls of the slain, and to make large money payments to their heirs—York gave the young Duke of Somerset and his mother five thousand marks, and Warwick made over one thousand to the young Clifford. After this curious bargain had been made, and a proclamation issued to the effect that both the victors and the vanquished of St. Albans had acted as true liegemen of the King, a solemn ceremony of reconciliation was held. The King walked in state to St. Paul's, behind him came the Queen, led by the Duke of York; then followed Salisbury hand in hand with Somerset, Warwick hand in hand with the Duke of Exeter, and after them their respective adherents two and two. The sight must have gladdened the King's kindly heart, but no one save his own guileless self could have supposed that such a reconciliation was final; almost the whole of his train were destined to die by each other's hands. The Queen and Somerset were one day to behead York and Salisbury; Warwick was destined to slay Exeter's son; and so all down the long procession.

As one of the tokens of reconciliation, Warwick was created "Chief Captain to guard the Sea," a post wherein centred the ambition of his unwilling partner in the great procession, the Duke of Exeter. The office was not one with many attractions. The royal navy comprised no more than the Grace Dieu and two or three more large carracks. When a fleet was required, it was made up by requisitioning hastily-armed merchant-vessels from the maritime towns. Of late years, whenever such an array was mustered, the sailors had gone unpaid, and the command had been entrusted to some unskilled leader from the ranks of the Court party. England had entirely ceased to count as a naval power; her coasts were frequently ravaged by French expeditions, such as that which had burnt Sandwich in 1457, and pirates and privateers of all nations swarmed in the Channel.

In his capacity as Captain of Calais, Warwick had been compelled to learn something of the Channel, but we should never have guessed that he had accumulated enough of the seaman's craft to make him a competent admiral. Nevertheless, his doings during the twenty months of his command at sea entitle him to a respectable place by the side of Blake and Monk and our other inland-bred naval heroes. He not merely acquired enough skill to take the charge of a fleet in one of the rough and ready sea-fights of the day, but actually became a competent seaman. At a pinch, as he showed a few years later, he could himself take the tiller and pilot his ship for a considerable voyage.

The tale of Warwick's first naval venture has been most fortunately preserved to us by the letter of an actor in it.

On Trinity Sunday (May 28th) in the morning [writes John Jernyngan] came tidings unto my Lord of Warwick that there were twenty-eight sail of Spaniards on the sea, whereof sixteen were great ships of forecastle; and then my Lord went and manned five ships of forecastle and three carvells and four pinnaces, and on the Monday we met together before Calais at four of the clock in the morning, and fought together till ten. And there we took six of their ships, and they slew of our men about fourscore and hurt two hundred of us right sore. And we slew of them about twelvescore, and hurt a five hundred of them. It happed that at the first boarding of them we took a ship of three hundred tons, and I was left therein and twenty-three men with me. And they fought so sore that our men were fain to leave them. Then came they and boarded the ship that I was in, and there was I taken, and was prisoner with them six hours, and was delivered again in return for their men that were taken at the first. As men say, there has not been so great a battle upon the sea these forty winters. And, to say sooth, we were well and truly beaten: so my Lord has sent for more ships, and is like to fight them again in haste.

Such a hard-fought struggle against superior numbers was almost as honorable to Warwick's courage and enterprise as a victory, and the indomitable pluck which he displayed seems to have won the hearts of the sailors, who were ever after, down to the day of his death, faithful to his cause. But his later undertakings were fortunate as well as bold.

The best known of them took place in the spring of 1458. Sweeping the Channel with fourteen small vessels, Warwick came on five great ships—"three great Genoese carracks, and two Spaniards far larger and higher than the others." For two days Warwick fought a running fight with the enemy, "hard and long, for he had no vessel that could compare in size with theirs." Finally he took three of the carracks and put the other two to flight.

Nearly a thousand Spaniards were slain, and the prisoners were so many that the prisons of Calais could hardly contain them. The prizes were richly laden, and their contents were valued at no less than £10,000. The markets of Calais and Kent were for the moment so charged with Southern goods that a shilling bought that year more than two would have bought the year before.

This fight naturally made Warwick popular with merchants and sailors, but it was less liked at Westminster; for although at odds with the King of Castile, England was not at this moment engaged in hostilities with the Genoese, though there was a dispute in progress about the ill-treatment of some British merchants by them. Another feat of Warwick's, however, was to get him into worse trouble. Early in the autumn of the same year he had an engagement in the Straits of Dover with a great fleet of Hanseatic vessels from Lubeck, who were sailing southward to France. From them he took five ships which he brought into Calais. Now England had signed a commercial treaty with the Hansa only two years before, and this engagement was a flagrant violation of it. It led Warwick's enemies on the Continent to call him no better than a pirate. What was his plea of justification we do not know. It may be, as some have alleged, that he mistook the Germans at first for Spaniards or Frenchmen. It may be that he fell out with them on some question as to the rights of the English admiral in the narrow seas, such as gave constant trouble in later centuries, and were the forerunners of the famous quarrels over the "right of search" and "the right of salute."

But about Warwick's capture of the Hanseatic vessels there was no doubt. A month later a board was appointed, consisting of Lord

Rivers, Sir Thomas Kyrriel, and seven other members, to investigate the matter.

On November 8th Warwick came over from Calais to lay his defence before the King and Council. Henry received him courteously enough, and there was much sage talk about the marches of Picardy, "but the Earl could judge well enough by the countenances of many who sat in the Council Chamber that they bore him hatred, so that he bethought him of the warnings that his father had lately written him about the Queen's friends."

Next day when Warwick again came into the royal presence, the Council had hardly begun when a great tumult arose in the court, "the noise was heard over the whole palace, and every one was calling for Warwick." What had happened was, that the retainers of Somerset and Wiltshire had fallen on the Earl's attendants and were making an end of them. Warwick ran down to see what was the matter, but the moment that he appeared in the court he was set on by a score of armed men, and it was only by the merest chance that he was able to cut his way down to the water-stairs, and leap with two of his men into a boat. He escaped with his life to the Surrey side, but his followers were not so lucky; three were slain and many wounded.

Warwick declared that the whole business had been a deliberate plot to murder him, and he was probably right; but the lords of the Queen's party maintained that the affray had been a chance medley between the two bands of retainers, and that the first blow had been struck by one of Warwick's men. But whatever was the truth about the matter, Warwick could not be blamed if he swore never to come to Court again without armed men at his heels. The sequel of the quarrel shows what had really been intended. Next day the Queen and her friends represented to the King that the quarrel had been due to brawling on Warwick's part, and procured an order for committing him to the Tower. Warned of this by a secret friend in the Council, the Earl rode off in haste to Warwick Castle, and sent to his father and the Duke of York. The three held a conference, in which they resolved that at the next hostile move of their enemies they would repeat the line of conduct which had been so successful four years before—they would muster their retainers and deliver the King by force out of the hands of the Court party.

Meanwhile Warwick retired to Calais, where he called together the officers of the garrison, and the Mayor and aldermen, set forth to them the attempt upon his life, and begged them to be true to him and guard him against the machination of his enemies.

The next attack of the Queen on the followers of York was long in coming; nine months elapsed between the affray at Westminster and the final outbreak of Civil War.

Meanwhile [says the chronicler] the realm of England was out of all good governance, as it had been many days before; for the King was simple, and led by covetous counsel, and owed more than he was worth. His debts encreased daily, but payment was there none; for all the manors and lordships that pertained to the Crown the King had given away, so that he had almost nought to live on. And such impositions as were put on the people, as taxes, tallages, and 'fifteenths,' all were spent in vain, for the King held no household and maintained no wars. So for these misgovernances the hearts of the people were turned from them that had the land in governance, and their blessing was turned to cursing. The Queen and her affinity ruled the realm as they liked, gathering riches innumerable. The officers of the realm, and specially the Earl of Wiltshire, the Treasurer, for to enrich themselves pilled the poor people, and disherited rightful heirs, and did many wrongs. The Queen was sore defamed, and many said that he that was called the Prince was not the King's son, but gotten in adultery.

The name of Wiltshire, "the best-favoured knight in the land, and the most feared of losing his beauty," was united with that of Margaret by many tongues, and the Queen's behaviour was certainly curious; for instead of staying with her husband, she was continually absent from his side, busied in all manner of political intrigues, and only visiting King Henry when some grant or signature had to be wrung out of him. All the summer of 1459 she was in Lancashire and Cheshire "allying to her the knights and squires in those parts for to have their benevolence, and held open household among them, and made her son give a livery blazoned with a swan to all the gentlemen of the country, trusting through their strength to make her son King; for she was making privy means to some lords of England for to stir the King to resign the crown to his son; but she could not bring her purpose about."

The exact details of the outbreak of the war are hard to arrange chronologically. Writs were being sent about by the Queen in the King's name ordering every one to be ready to assemble "with as many men as they might, defensibly arrayed," as early as May. But no such muster seems to have taken place, and it was not till September that a blow was struck. In the middle of that month an army was raised in the Midlands with which the King took the field. A summons was then sent to Salisbury, who lay at Sherif

Hoton in his northern lands, bidding him come to London. Remembering what had happened to his son on his last visit to the King, Salisbury went not, but took the summons, combined with the mustering of the King's forces, as an alarm of war. Collecting some three thousand of his Yorkshire tenants, he marched off to seek his brother-in-law York, who was lying at Ludlow. At the same time he sent messengers to his son at Calais, bidding him cross over at once to join him.

Warwick, seeing that the crisis was come, took two hundred men-at-arms and four hundred archers of the garrison of Calais, under Sir Andrew Trollope a veteran of the French War, and crossed to Sandwich. He left Calais, where lay his wife and his two daughters, in charge of his uncle, William Neville Lord Fauconbridge, "a little man in stature but a knight of great reverence." Warwick marched quietly through London, and crossed the Midlands as far as Coleshill in Warwickshire without meeting an enemy. There he just avoided a battle, for Somerset, with a great force from his Wessex lands, was marching through the town from south-west to north-east the same day that Warwick traversed it from south-east to north-west; but as it happened they neither of them caught any sight or heard any rumour of the other.

While Warwick was taking his way through the Midlands, decisive events had been occurring. When the Queen, who lay at Eccleshall in Staffordshire, heard that Salisbury was on his way to York's castle of Ludlow, she called out all her new-made friends of the north-west Midlands, and bade them intercept the Earl. Lord Audley their leader was given a commission to arrest Salisbury and send him to the Tower of London. All the knighthood of

Cheshire and Shropshire came together and joined Audley, who was soon at the head of nearly ten thousand men. With this force he threw himself across Salisbury's path at Blore Heath near Market Drayton on September 23rd. The old Earl refused to listen to Audley's summons to surrender, entrenched himself on the edge of a wood and waited to be attacked. Audley first led two cavalry charges against the Yorkist line, and when these were beaten back by the arrows of the northern archers, launched a great column of billmen and dismounted knights against the enemy. After hard fighting it was repulsed, Audley himself was slain, and the Lancastrians drew back, "leaving dead on the field most of those notable knights and squires of Chesshire that had taken the badge of the Swan."

In the night Salisbury drew off his men and marched round the defeated enemy, who still lay in front of his position. A curious story is told of his retreat by the chronicler Gregory. "Next day," he says, "the Earl of Salisbury, if he had stayed, would have been taken, so great were the forces that would have been brought up by the Queen, who lay at Eccleshall only six miles from the field." But the enemy knew nothing of Salisbury's departure, "because an Austin friar shot guns all night in the park at the rear of the field, so that they knew not the Earl was departed. Next morrow they found neither man nor child in that park save the friar, and he said that it was for fear that he abode in that park, firing the guns to keep up his heart."

Salisbury was now able to join York at Ludlow without further molestation, and Warwick came in a few days later without having seen an enemy. The Duke and the younger Earl called out their vassals of the Welsh March, and their united forces soon amounted to twenty thousand men. They made no hostile movement however, though the Lancastrian force defeated at Blore Heath was now being joined by new reinforcements and lay opposite them in great strength. But the Duke and the two Earls went forward to Worcester, and there in the cathedral took a solemn oath that they meant nothing against the King's estate or the common weal of the realm. They charged the Prior of Worcester and Dr. William Lynwood to lay before the King a declaration "that they would forbear and avoid all things that might serve to the effusion of Christian blood," and would not strike a blow except in self-defence, being only in arms to save their own lives.

The refusal of the Yorkist lords to assume the offensive, if creditable to their honesty, was fatal to their cause. For the next three weeks the levies of Northern and Central England came pouring into the Queen's camp, and the King himself, waking up for once, assumed the command in person. A curious record in the preamble of an Act of Parliament of this year tells us how he buckled on his armour, "and spared not for any impediment or difficulty of way, nor intemperance of weather, but jeopardied his royal person, and continued his labour for thirty days, and sometimes lodged in the bare field for two nights together, with all his host, in the cold season of the year, not resting in the same place more than one night save only on the Sundays." About October 12th, the King, whose army now amounted to as many as fifty thousand men, pushed slowly forward on to Ludlow, putting out as he went strongly-worded proclamations which stigmatised the Duke and the Earls as traitors, and summoned their followers to disperse, promising free pardon to all save Salisbury and the others who had fought at Blore Heath.

York and Warwick had, of course, no intention of abandoning their kinsman; they paid no heed to the royal proclamation, but they soon found that their followers were far from holding it so lightly. The Yorkists were so manifestly inferior in numbers to the enemy, less than half their force indeed, that the men's hearts were failing them. Their position on the Welsh Border, with the King's army cutting them off from England, and with the Welsh in arms behind them, was unsatisfactory, and none of the Yorkist barons had succeeded in joining them except Lord Clinton and Lord Grey of Powis. The inaction of their leaders had allowed them time to think over their position, and it would appear that the news of the King's proclamation had reached them, and the announcement of pardon worked its effect. York seems to have recognised that the use of the royal name against him was the fatal thing, and proceeded to spread a rumour through his camp that King Henry was really dead. He even ordered his chaplains to celebrate the mass for the dead in the midst of the camp. But the stratagem recoiled on his head next day, when the truth became known, and the King was seen, with his banner displayed at his side, leading forward in person the van of the Lancastrian army. At nightfall on October 13th the armies were only separated by the Teme, then in flood and covering the fields for some way on each side of its course. The Duke set some cannon to play upon the King's line, but the darkness or the distance kept them from doing any hurt. This was all the fighting that was destined to take place.

That night demoralisation set in among the Yorkist ranks. It commenced with the veteran Trollope, who secretly led off his six hundred Calais troops from their place in the Yorkist line and joined the enemy. Lord Powis followed his example, and at dawn the whole army was melting away. York bade the bridges be broken down, and began to draw off, but nothing could keep his men together; they were dispersing with such rapidity that he could no longer hope to fight. Accordingly he bade those who still followed him to save themselves, and made off with his two sons Edward and Edmund, Warwick and Salisbury, and a few devoted retainers, to seek some place of refuge.

Thus by the Rout of Ludford all the work of Blore Heath and St. Albans was entirely undone.

Chapter 8

WARWICK IN EXILE

The adventures of Warwick after the army of York broke up have luckily been preserved to us in some detail. He and his father, together with the Duke and his two sons Edward and Edmund, fled southwards together with a few score of horse, hotly pursued by Sir Andrew Trollope and his men. So close was the chase that John and Thomas Neville, who lingered behind their brother and father—both having been wounded at Blore Heath—were taken prisoners. Presently the party was forced to break up by the imminence of their peril. The Duke of York and his second son Edmund turned off into Wales, with the design of taking ship for Ireland. Salisbury, Warwick, and Edward Plantagenet, the young Earl of March, York's eldest son and Salisbury's god-child and nephew, accompanied by Sir John Dynham and only two persons more, fled across Herefordshire by cross-roads, avoiding the towns, and then by a hazardous journey through Gloucestershire and Somersetshire reached the coast of Devon, apparently somewhere near Barnstaple. There the fugitives turned into a fishing village, where Sir John Dynham bought for two hundred and twenty-two nobles—the sum of the party's resources—a one-masted fishing-smack. He gave out that he was bound for Bristol, and hired a master and four hands to navigate the little vessel.

When they had got well out from land Warwick asked the master if he knew the seas of Cornwall and the English Channel. The man answered that he was quite ignorant of them, and had never rounded the Land's End. "Then all that company was much cast down: but the Earl seeing that his father and the rest were sad, said to them that by the favour of God and St. George he would himself steer them to a safe port. And he stripped to his doublet, and took the helm himself, and had the sail hoisted, and turned the ship's bows westward," much to the disgust, we doubt not, of the master and his four hands, who had not counted on such a voyage when they hired themselves to sail to Bristol town.

It was not for nothing that Warwick had ranged the Channel for two years. He now proved that he was a competent seaman, by navigating the little vessel down the Bristol Channel, round the Land's End, and across to Guernsey. Here they were eight days wind-bound, but putting forth on the ninth ran safely up the Channel and came ashore at Calais on November 3rd, just twenty days after the rout of Ludford. Counting the crew, they had been eleven souls in the vessel.

Warwick found Calais still safe in the hands of his uncle Fauconbridge, whom he had left in charge of the town and of his own wife and daughters when he went to England two months before. Overjoyed at the news, Fauconbridge came to meet him on the quay, and fell on his neck. "Then all those lords went together in pilgrimage to Notre Dame de St. Pierre, and gave thanks for their safety. And when they came into Calais, the Mayor and the aldermen and the merchants of the Staple came out to meet them, and made them good cheer. And that night they were merry enough, when they thought they might have found Calais already in the hands of their enemies."

Such indeed might well have been their fortune, for the Duke of Somerset was already at Sandwich, with some hundreds of men-at-arms. The King had appointed him Captain of Calais, and he was on his way to remove Fauconbridge and get the town into his own keeping. But the south-west wind which blew Warwick up from Guernsey had kept Somerset on shore.

That very evening the wind shifted, and late at night Somerset's herald appeared before the water-gate to warn the garrison that his master would arrive to take command next day. "Then the guard answered the herald that they would give his news to the Earl of Warwick, who was their sole and only captain, and that he should have Warwick's answer in a few minutes. The herald was much abashed, and got him away, and went back that same night to his master."

No one in England knew what had become of Warwick or Salisbury, and Somerset's surprise was as great as his wrath when he found that they had anticipated him at Calais. Next morning he set sail with his forces, of which the greater part were comprised of Sir Andrew Trollope's soldiers, making for Guisnes, with the intention of attacking Calais from the land side. But a tempest rose up while he was at sea, and though he and most of his men came ashore at Guisnes, the vessels that contained their horses and stores and armour were driven into Calais harbour for safety, and compelled to surrender to Warwick. The Earl "thanked Providence for the present, and not the Duke of Somerset," and was much pleased at the chance, for his men were greatly in want of arms. He had the prisoners forth, and went down their ranks; then he picked out those that had been officers under him and had sworn the oath to him as Captain of Calais and threw them into prison, but the rest he sent away in safety, saying that they had but served their King to the best of their knowledge; only Lord Audley, Somerset's second in command, son to the peer whom Salisbury had slain at Blore Heath, was not permitted to depart, and was consigned to the castle. But the men who had broken their oath to Warwick were brought out into the market-place next day, and beheaded before a great concourse of the citizens.

Somerset and Sir Andrew Trollope had been received into Guisnes, and made it their headquarters. But for some time they could do nothing against Calais, because they were in want of arms and horses. It was not till they had got themselves refitted by help of the French of Boulogne that they were able to harm Warwick. Meanwhile they were practically cut off from England, for Warwick's ships held the straits, and neither news nor men came across to them. Presently Somerset set to work to intercept Warwick's supply of provisions, which was drawn mainly from Flanders, and the Earl had to arrange that every market-day parties of the garrison should ride out to escort the Flemings and their waggons. It might have gone hard with Calais if this source of supply had been cut off, but Warwick had concluded a secret agreement with Duke Philip, by which the introduction of food into the town was to be winked at by the Flemish officials, notwithstanding any treaties with England that might exist. Neither Somerset nor Warwick got much profit out of the continual skirmishes that resulted from the attempts of the Lancastrians to cut off the waggon-trains from Dunkirk and Gravelines.

So passed the months of November and December 1459, with no stirring incidents but plenty of bickering. But Christmastide brought with it abundant excitement: the Queen had at last taken measures to reinforce Somerset, and Lord Rivers with his son Sir Antony Woodville had come down to Sandwich with a few hundred men to take the first safe opportunity of crossing to Guisnes. But the time was stormy and the troops mutinous; they got little or no pay, and scattered themselves over the neighbourhood to live at free quarters, so that Rivers lay in Sandwich almost unattended.

"So at Christmastide the Earl called together his men-at-arms, and asked whether it was not possible to get back his great ship that he had used when he was admiral, for it lay at Sandwich in Lord Rivers' hands with several ships more. And Sir John Dynham answered 'yea,' and swore to take it back with God's aid if the Earl would give him four hundred men to sail with him. So the Earl bade his men arm, and fitted out his vessels, and he gave the charge of the business to Sir John Dynham, and Sir John Wenlock that wise knight, who had done many feats of arms in his day." They set out at night, and arrived off Sandwich before dawn. Waiting for the tide to rise, they ran into the harbour at five in the morning. No one paid any attention to them, for the men of Sandwich thought they were but timber-ships from the Baltic, as all the men-at-arms were kept below hatches.

There was no stir in the town, and Wenlock was able to seize the ships and fit them out in haste, while Dynham swept the streets and caught Lord Rivers' men-at-arms as they turned out to see what was the matter. Sir Antony Woodville was captured one hour later, as he rode into the town from London, whither he had gone to ask the Queen for a supply of money. Lord Rivers himself was found, still asleep, in his bed at the Black Friars, and carried on board his own ship before he could realise what was happening.

The men of Sandwich, like the rest of the Kentishmen, had no desire to harm the Yorkists, so that there was no fighting, and Dynham and Wenlock sailed home at their ease, without striking a single blow, with their prisoners and all the war-ships in the port save the Grace Dieu alone, which was found quite unready for the sea.

That evening they were again in Calais, and landed in triumph to deliver their spoils to Warwick. A quaint and undignified scene followed when the prisoners were brought out. "So that evening Lord Rivers and his son were taken before the three Earls, accompanied by a hundred and sixty torches. And first the Earl of Salisbury rated Lord Rivers, calling him a knave's son, that he should have been so rude as to call him and these other lords traitors, for they should be found the King's true lieges when he should be found a traitor indeed. And then my Lord of Warwick rated him, and said that his father was but a squire, and that he had made himself by his marriage, and was but a made lord, so that it was not his part to hold such language of lords of the King's blood. And then my Lord of March rated him in like wise. Lastly Sir Antony was rated for his language of all three lords in the same manner."

If Rivers had any sense of humour, he must have felt the absurdity of being rated by the Nevilles—who more than any other race in England had risen by a series of wealthy alliances—for having "made himself by his marriage." But probably anger and fear were sufficient to keep him from any such reflections. We could wish that Warwick had been less undignified in the hour of his triumph; but if his words were rough his actions were not: Rivers and his son were sent to join Lord Audley in the castle, but they were well treated in their captivity and came to no harm. Before many months were out they joined their captor's cause.

It would have been hard for the actors in the scene to foresee the changes that ten years were to make in their relations to each other. By 1470 Rivers was destined to find himself the father-in-law of the young Earl of March, who was now exercising his tongue against him in imitation of the Nevilles, and to lose his life in the service of the house of York. Warwick, on the other hand, was to become the deadly enemy of the young Prince whom he was now harbouring and training to arms, and to adopt the Lancastrian cause which Rivers had deserted.

The months of January and February passed in continual skirmishing with Somerset and the garrison of Guisnes, which led to no marked result; but about the beginning of Lent news arrived at Calais that the Duke of York, of whom nothing definite had been heard since October, was now in great force in Ireland, where he had got possession of Dublin, "and was greatly strengthened by the earls and homagers of that country." Warwick at once resolved to sail to Ireland to concert measures with his uncle, and to learn if it would be possible to invade England; for it was obvious that unless some vigorous offensive action were taken in the spring, the Lancastrians would finally succeed in bringing enough men across to form the siege of Calais, and then the town could not hold out for ever.

Accordingly, though the storms of March were at their highest, Warwick equipped his ten largest ships, manned them with one thousand five hundred sailors and men-at-arms, "the best stuff in Calais," and sailed down the Channel for Ireland. The voyage was undisturbed by the enemy, but terribly tempestuous and protracted. However, the Earl reached Waterford at last, and found there not only York and his son Rutland, but his own mother, the Countess of Salisbury, who had fled over to Ireland when she heard that her name was inserted among the list of persons attainted by the Lancastrian Parliament which met at Leicester in December 1459.

Warwick found the Duke in good spirits, and so hopeful that he was ready to engage to land in Wales in June with all the force that could be raised in Ireland, if Warwick would promise to head a descent on Kent at the same moment. This plan was agreed upon, and the Earl set sail to return about May 1st, taking with him his mother, who was anxious to rejoin her husband whom she had not seen for nearly a year.

Meanwhile the news of Warwick's departure for Ireland had reached the Lancastrian government, and the Duke of Exeter, Warwick's successor in the office of admiral, had sworn to prevent him from returning to Calais. Accordingly Exeter "with the great ship called the Grace Dieu, and three great carracks, and ten other ships all well armed and ordered," was now besetting the Channel. When Warwick was off Start Point the vessel which sailed in advance of his squadron to reconnoitre the way returned in haste, with the news that a squadron was lying off Dartmouth and that some fishing-boats, with whom communication had been held, reported the Duke of Exeter to be in command.

Warwick was resolved to fight, though the enemy was considerably superior in force. He sent for his captains on board his carvel "and prayed that they would serve him loyally that day, for he had good hope that God would give him the victory," to which they answered that they were well disposed enough for a fight and that the men were in good heart. Accordingly the Earl's ten ships formed line and bore down on the Duke's fourteen. A fight appeared imminent, when suddenly the whole Lancastrian fleet went about, and fled in disorder into Dartmouth harbour, which lay just behind them. This unexpected action was caused by mutiny on board. When the Duke had given orders to prepare for action, his officers had come to him in dismay, to announce that the men would not arm to fight their old commander, and that if he came any nearer to the Earl, the crews would undoubtedly rise and deliver them over to the enemy. Accordingly Exeter gave orders to retire into harbour.

Warwick, however, could not know of the cause of the enemy's retreat, and having a good west wind behind him and a great desire to get back to Calais, from which he had now been absent more than ten weeks, pursued his journey without attempting anything against Dartmouth. He reached Calais in safety on June 1st, and was proud to restore his mother, "who had suffered grievously from the sea during her voyage," to his father's arms. Salisbury and Fauconbridge had been much alarmed at the length of his absence, and the more faint-hearted of the garrison had begun to murmur that he had deserted them for good, and had fled to foreign parts to save his own person.

Now, however, all was stir and bustle in Calais, for Salisbury and Fauconbridge thoroughly approved of the plan of invasion which had been concerted at Dublin. The news from England indeed was all that could be desired. The reckless attainting of all the Yorkists by the Parliament of Leicester had met with grave disapproval. The retainers of the Lancastrian lords had been committing all sorts of misdoings, chief among which was the unprovoked sack of the town of Newbury by the followers of Ormond Earl of Wiltshire. London was murmuring savagely at the execution of seven citizens who, in company with a gentleman of the house of Neville, had been caught in the Thames on their way to Calais to join the Earls. The "unlearned preachers" whom the Government put up to preach against York at Paul's Cross were hooted down by the mob. The Commons of Kent were signifying in no doubtful terms their willingness to join the Earls, the moment that the banner of the White Rose should be unfurled in England. A fragment of a ballad hung by an unknown hand on the gate of Canterbury in June is worth quoting as an expression of their feelings.

> Send home, most gracious Jesu most benigne,
> Send home the true blood to his proper vein,
> Richard Duke of York thy servant insigne,
> Whom Satan not ceaseth to set at disdain,
> But by thee preserved he may not be slain.
> Set him 'ut sedeat in principibus' as he did before,
> And so to our new song Lord thyne ear incline,

> Gloria, laus et honor tibi sit Christe redemptor!
>
> Edward the Earl of March, whose fame the earth shall spread,
> Richard Earl of Salisbury, named Prudence,
> With that noble knight and flower of manhood
> Richard Earl of Warwick, shield of our defence,
> Also little Faulconbridge, a knight of grete reverence,
> Jesu! restore them to the honour they had before!

Nor was it only the Commons that were ready to join in a new appeal to arms. The partisans of York among the great houses, who had not definitely committed themselves at the time of the rout of Ludford, and so had escaped arrest and attainder, let it be known at Calais that they were ready for action. Chief among them were the Duke of Norfolk and the two brothers Lord Bourchier and Bourchier Archbishop of Canterbury, who pledged themselves to put their retainers in motion the moment that Warwick should cross the sea.

It was in no spirit of recklessness then that Warwick resolved to cross into Kent in the last week of June, with every man that could be spared from Calais. As a preliminary to his advance, he had resolved to clear away the only Lancastrian force that was watching him—a body of five hundred men-at-arms which had been sent down to Sandwich, to replace Lord Rivers' troops and to endeavour to communicate with Somerset at Guisnes. This body was commanded by Osbert Mundeford, one of the officers of the Calais garrison who had deserted Warwick in company with Sir Andrew Trollope.

Accordingly, on June 25th Sir John Dynham, the captor of Rivers, sailed over to Sandwich for the second time, and fell on Mundeford's force. There was a hot skirmish, for on this occasion the Lancastrians were not caught sleeping; but again the Yorkists won the day. Dynham indeed was wounded by a shot from a bombard, but his men stormed the town, routed the enemy, and took Mundeford prisoner. He was sent over to Calais, where he was tried for deserting his captain, as the prisoners of November 3rd had been, and beheaded next day outside the walls.

On the 27th Warwick himself, his father, the Earl of March, Lord Fauconbridge, Wenlock, and the rest of the leaders at Calais, crossed over to Sandwich with two thousand men in good array, leaving in the town the smallest garrison that could safely be trusted with the duty of keeping out Somerset. They had published before their landing a manifesto, which set out the stereotyped Yorkist grievances once more—the weak government, the crushing taxes, the exclusion of the King's relatives from his Council, the diversion of the revenue into the pockets of the courtiers, the misdoings of individual Lancastrian chiefs, the oppression of the King's lieges, and all the other customary complaints.

The three Earls had only been in Sandwich a few hours when, as had been agreed, the Archbishop of Canterbury came to join them with many of the tenants of the see arrayed in arms. They then moved forward, with numbers increasing at every step, for the Kentishmen came to meet them by thousands, and no one raised a hand against them.

The Lancastrians had been caught wholly unprepared. They seem to have been expecting raids from Warwick on the eastern coast, not on the southern, and except Mundeford's routed force there was no one in arms south of the Thames. The King and Queen were at Coventry, and most of the Lancastrian lords scattered each in their own lands. Lord Scales and Lord Hungerford were in command of London, where there were present a few other notables—Lord Vesey, Lord Lovell, and John de Foix titular Earl of Kendal. These leaders endeavoured to fortify the city, posting guns on London Bridge and placing their retainers in the Tower. But the aspect of the citizens was threatening, and Warwick was known to be coming on fast. The landing had taken place on the 27th, and on July 1st the three Earls and the Archbishop of Canterbury were already before the walls of London. They had marched over seventy miles in four days, taking the route of Canterbury, Rochester, and Dartford, and were at hand long before they were expected.

When the Archbishop's herald summoned the town there was some attempt made by the Lancastrian lords to offer resistance, but the mob rose and drove them into the Tower, while a deputation of aldermen went forth to offer a free entry to the Yorkist army.

On July 2nd the three Earls entered London in state, conducted by the Archbishop and a Papal Legate, a certain Bishop of Teramo who had been sent by Pius the Second to endeavour to reconcile the English factions and to get them to join in a crusade. He had allowed himself to be talked over by Warwick, and did all in his power to further the cause of York.

The Earls rode to St. Paul's and there before a great multitude, both clerical and lay, Warwick "recited the cause of their coming in to the land, how they had been put out from the King's presence with great violence, so that they might not come to his Highness to excuse themselves of the accusations laid against them. But now they were come again, by God's mercy, accompanied by their people, for to come into his presence, there to declare their innocence, or else to die upon the field. And there he made an oath upon the Cross of Canterbury, that they bore true faith and liegeance to the King's person, whereof he took Christ and His Holy Mother and all the Saints of Heaven to witness." We shall see that this last promise was not an entirely unmeaning formula in Warwick's mouth, and that his oath was not like the deliberate perjuries to which others of his contemporaries—notably Edward the Fourth—were prone.

Chapter 9

VICTORY AND DISASTER—NORTHAMPTON AND ST. ALBANS

When the arrival of the three Earls in London was known, all the Yorkist peers who were within touch of London came flocking in with their retainers. Thither came Warwick's uncle Edward Neville Lord Abergavenny, and his brother George Neville Bishop of Exeter, and his cousin Lord Scrope, and Clinton one of the victors of St. Albans, and Bourchier and Cobham and Say, and the Bishops of Ely, Salisbury, and Rochester. It is strange to read that Audley, who had been Warwick's prisoner in Calais ever since last November, also joined the Yorkists in arms. He had come to terms with his captor, and had agreed to forget the death of his father at Blore Heath and to serve the cause of York. In a few days an army of more than thirty thousand men had been gathered together.

The first task of the Yorkists was to provide for the blockade of the Tower of London, where Hungerford and Scales abode in great wrath, "shooting wild-fire into the town every hour, and laying great ordnance against it." Salisbury agreed to remain in charge of the city and to undertake the siege. With him were left Lord Cobham, Sir John Wenlock, and the greater part of the levy of London, commanded by the Lord Mayor and by one Harrow, a mercer. They brought batteries to bear on the Tower from the side of St. Katherine's wharf, "so they skirmished together daily, and much harm was done."

Meanwhile Warwick and the young Earl of March set out on Saturday July 5th, having with them the other Yorkist lords, "and much people out of Kent, Sussex, and Essex with much great ordnance." Marching by the great north road, past St. Albans and Towcester, they made for Northampton, where they heard that the King was collecting his host.

The invasion of England had been so sudden and its success so rapid that the Lancastrians had not had time to call in all their strength, more especially as it lay to a great extent in the extreme North and West. But the Midlands were well roused, and, if a Yorkist chronicler is to be believed, the Queen "had it proclaimed in Cheshire and Lancashire that if so the King had the victory of the Earls, then every man should take what he might, and make havoc in Kent, Essex, Middlesex, Surrey, and Sussex." The Duke of Buckingham had the chief command, though he was not of the Court party nor a great lover of the Queen's, but out of sheer loyalty he now—as formerly at St. Albans—came out with all his retainers when he received the King's missive. With him were Egremont and Beaumont, both deadly enemies of the Nevilles and favourites of the Queen, the Earl of Shrewsbury, Lord Grey de Ruthyn, and many more. Their forces, though very considerable, were still somewhat inferior to those of the Yorkists.

The King's camp was pitched just outside Northampton town, in the meadows south of the Nen, near the Nunnery between Sandiford and Hardingstone. The position had been strongly entrenched, and the earthworks were lined with a numerous artillery; the river covered both flanks, the lines being drawn from point to point in a broad bend of its course.

Warwick, in accordance with his declaration at St. Paul's on the previous Thursday, made three separate attempts to secure permission to approach the King's person; but Buckingham sternly refused to listen to his envoys, the Bishops of Rochester and Salisbury. "You came here not as bishops to treat of peace, but as men-at-arms," he said, pointing to the squadrons arrayed under the bishops' banners in the Yorkist host. Negotiations were fruitless, and at two in the afternoon Warwick drew out his army on the rising ground by the old Danish camp, the Hunsborough, which overlooks the water-meadows, and descended to the attack. Fauconbridge led the vanguard on the left, the Earl himself the centre, Edward of March, now seeing his first stricken field, conducted the right wing. Before the attack it was proclaimed that every man should spare the Commons, and slay none but the knights and lords, with whom alone lay the blame for the shedding of all the blood that might fall that day.

The first assault on the Lancastrian lines failed completely. The obstacles were far greater than Warwick had imagined; it was six feet from the bottom of the ditch to the top of the rampart, and the trenches were full of water, for it had rained heavily in the morning. How the day would have gone if treachery had not come to the succour of the Yorkists it is impossible to say; but only a few minutes after the first gun had been fired, Lord Grey de Ruthyn on the Lancastrian left mounted the badge of the Ragged Staff, and his men were seen beckoning to the Yorkists to approach, and leaning over the rampart to reach their hands to pull them up. Assisted in this way, the Earl of March's column got within the entrenchments, and sweeping along their front cleared a space for Warwick to burst in. All was over in half an hour and with very little bloodshed. Only three hundred men fell, but among them were nearly all the Lancastrian leaders. On foot and in their heavy armour the lords and knights could not get away. The aged Buckingham fell at the door of his own tent, and Beaumont, Egremont, and Shrewsbury close to the King's quarters, as they strove to protect his retreat. But the King, helpless as ever, was too late to fly, and fell into the hands of an archer named Henry Montford. His capture, however, was not so important so long as his wife and child remained at large; and Margaret—as adroit as her husband was shiftless—was already speeding away with the young Prince, bound for North Wales.

Warwick and March conducted King Henry back with all respect to London, where he was lodged in the palace at Westminster. They had done their work so rapidly that they had not needed the assistance of the Duke of York, whose arrival from Ireland—he was two months later than his promise—was just announced from the West. Even before he appeared the victors of Northampton had begun to reconstitute the King's ministry. Henry was made to sign patents appointing Salisbury Lieutenant in the six northern counties; his son, George Bishop of Exeter, received the Chancellorship; John Neville another son was made the King's Chamberlain, and Lord Bourchier got the Treasury. Warwick himself was re-established de jure in the position he had been so long holding de facto, the captainship of Calais.

The garrison of the Tower of London surrendered nine days after the battle of Northampton. Most of the defenders went away in safety, but Lord Scales, who was much hated by the populace of

London, was not so fortunate. He took boat for the sanctuary of Westminster, but was recognised as he rowed along by some water-men, who gave chase to him and slew him on the river "just under the river wall of Winchester House." His body was stripped and thrown ashore into the cemetery of St. Mary Overy, whence it was removed and honourably buried by the Earls of March and Warwick that night. "Great pity was it that so noble a knight, so well approved in the wars of France and Normandy, should die so mischievously," adds the chronicler.

A Parliament was summoned by the Yorkists to meet on October 9th. Meanwhile Warwick was well employed. When August came round he ran across to Calais to see to his old antagonist at Guisnes. Somerset was now in low spirits, and willingly met the Earl at Newnham Bridge, there to be reconciled to him and make peace. But after he had embraced Warwick and assented to all his conditions, he secretly departed with his follower Trollope, fled through Picardy to Dieppe, and took refuge in his own south-western county. Meanwhile the Earl conducted his mother and wife in great state back to London, and re-established them in their old dwelling of "the Harbour." He spent September in going on a pilgrimage with the Countess to the shrine of the Virgin at Walsingham in Norfolk. On this journey he ran great peril, for Lord Willoughby, an unreconciled Lancastrian, lay in wait for him near Lichfield on his return, and was within an ace of making him prisoner.

So Warwick came at last to his own Midland estates. And there all the knights and ladies of his lands came to him "complaining of the evils that they had suffered in the past year from the Duke of

Somerset, who had pilled and robbed them, and sacked their towns and manors, and usurped the Earl's castles; but notwithstanding all their troubles they praised Heaven for the joyous return of their lord."

York had reached Chester early in September, and had marched slowly through his estates in the Welsh March towards London. When he came to Abingdon "he sent for trompeteres and claryners from London, and gave them banners with the royal arms of England without distinction or diversity, and commanded his sword to be borne upright before him, and so he rode till he came to the gates of the palace of Westminster." This assumption of royal state was the beginning of evils.

Meanwhile the Parliament was already sitting before the Duke's arrival. King Henry opened it with due solemnity, and heard it commence its work by repealing all the Acts of the Lancastrian Parliament of Leicester, and by removing the attainders of the Yorkist lords. On the third day of the session, Richard of York came up in the evening, and entered the palace, where he rudely took possession of the royal apartments. "He had the doors broken open, and King Henry hearing the great noise gave place, and took him another chamber that night."

This unceremonious eviction of his sovereign was only the beginning of the Duke's violent conduct. Next morning he went to the House of Lords, and approaching the throne laid his hand on the cushion as if about to take formal possession of the seat. Archbishop Bourchier asked him what he would do, and the Duke then made a lengthy reply "challenging and claiming the realm and crown of England as male heir of King Richard the Second, and proposing without any delay to be crowned on All Hallows' Day then following." The lords listened with obvious disapproval and dismay, and York did not even venture to seat himself on the throne. The meeting broke up without further transaction of business.

"Now when the Earl of Warwick, who had not been present that day, heard this, he was very wroth, and sent for the Archbishop and prayed him to go to the Duke and tell him that he was acting evilly, and to remind him of the many promises he had made to King Henry." Warwick in short remembered his oath of July 4th, and was determined that Henry should not be despoiled of his throne, but only placed in the hands of Yorkist ministers. The Archbishop refused to face the Duke.

Then the Earl sent for his brother Thomas Neville, and entered into his barge, and rowed to the palace. It was all full of the Duke's men-of-arms, but the Earl stayed not, and went straight to the Duke's chamber, and found him standing there, leaning against a side-board. And there were hard words between them, for the Earl told him that neither the lords nor the people would suffer him to strip the King of his crown. And as they wrangled, the Earl of Rutland came in and said to his cousin, "Fair sir be not angry, for you know that we have the true right to the crown, and that my Lord and Father here must have it." But the Earl of March his brother stayed him and said, "Brother, vex no man, for all shall be well." But the Earl of Warwick would stay no longer when he understood his uncle's intent, and went off hastily to his barge, greeting no one as he went save his cousin of March.

Next day, when his wrath had cooled down, the Earl sent to his uncle the Bishops of Ely and Rochester, Lord Audley, and a London citizen named Grey, to beg and beseech him to give up his enterprise. The Duke sent them away, with the answer that he would be crowned the very next Monday, the day of the translation of St. Edward the Confessor (October 13th). The preparations for the coronation were actually made, and the crowd was mustering in the Abbey, when on a last appeal made by Sir Thomas Neville in the name of his brother and of all the lords and commonalty of England, the Duke wavered. Fearing to offend his greatest supporters beyond redemption he temporised, put off his coronation, and began to negotiate.

Richard Neville, in fact, had matched his will against that of his imperious uncle and had won. The Duke was never crowned. The arrangement at which the parties arrived was that Henry should be King for life, that York should be made Protector, named Prince of Wales, Duke of Cornwall, and Earl of Chester, and should be acknowledged as heir to the crown. The Duke, on the other hand, swore to be faithful to the King so long as he should live. On All Saints' Day the agreement was solemnly ratified at St. Paul's, whither the lords went in procession, Warwick bearing the sword before the King, and Edward of March bearing the King's mantle. "And the crowd shouted 'Long live King Henry and the Earl of Warwick,' for the said Earl had the good voice of the people, because he knew how to give them fair words, showing himself easy and familiar with them, for he was very subtle at gaining his ends, and always spoke not of himself but of the augmentation and good governance of the kingdom, for which he would have spent his life: and thus he had the goodwill of England, so that in all the land he was the lord who was held in most esteem and faith and credence."

The Act of Parliament which recorded the agreement of York and King Henry made no mention of Queen Margaret or of the Prince her son. But it was of little use passing Acts of Parliament while she was at large and the Lancastrian lords of the North and West unsubdued. Margaret's first move had been to stir up the Scots, and at her bidding James the Second crossed the Border and laid siege to Roxburgh, which was then an English town. Fauconbridge, Warwick's uncle, was sent north to defend the place, but later events deprived him of aid from England, and he was forced to surrender, though not till after the King of Scots had fallen, slain by the bursting of one of his own siege guns.

But the Scotch invasion was only one of Margaret's schemes. Her main hope lay in a rising of the Lancastrians who had not suffered at Northampton; and from her retreat at Harlech in North Wales she sent to summon them together. Their mustering-place was in the North, where the Earl of Northumberland and Lord Neville, brother of Ralph Earl of Westmoreland, and Clifford son of the Clifford who fell at St. Albans, united their retainers as the nucleus of an army. To them fled Somerset, regardless of his oath at Calais, and Exeter the late Admiral, and Courtney Earl of Devon, and Willoughby and Roos and Hungerford, and many more.

The danger was so imminent that the Duke of York, after wearing the honours of the protectorate for no more than three weeks, resolved to march north and disperse the gathering of the

Queen's friends. He took with him his second son Edmund of Rutland, a boy of seventeen; Salisbury accompanied him, and he also left his first-born at home and went out with his fourth son Thomas Neville. The Duke and the Earl raised about six thousand men, and proceeded on their way, unopposed save by a small Lancastrian force which they beat at Worksop, till they reached Sandal Castle, one of York's family strongholds, close beside the town of Wakefield. When they arrived there, about Christmas Eve, they learnt that the Queen's army was much stronger than they had reckoned, and sent south for reinforcements. But on December 30th they were themselves assailed by forces tripling their own small host, under Somerset and Clifford. The Duke rashly fought in the open, though many of his men were scattered over the country-side foraging. It is said that he relied on help treacherously promised him by some of the Lancastrian leaders; but he was disappointed. No one played for his benefit the part that Grey de Ruthyn had carried out at Northampton.

The defeat of the Yorkists was decisive. Two thousand two hundred men out of their five thousand were slain. The fate of war fell heavily on the leaders, hardly one of whom escaped. The Duke fell on the field, with Thomas Neville and William Lord Harington. The Earl of Rutland, "the best-disposed young gentleman in England," was slain in the pursuit as he fled across Wakefield Bridge. Salisbury's fate was more unhappy still; he was taken prisoner, and beheaded next day at Pontefract by the Bastard of Exeter, "though he offered great sums of money that he should have grant of his life." The heads of Salisbury and his son, of Harington, and of five knights, were set on spikes over the gate of

York, with that of Duke Richard in the midst, crowned with a paper crown in mockery of the prospective kingship that he had never enjoyed.

All the Lancastrians of the North and the Midlands rose at once to join the Queen. She was soon at the head of forty thousand men, largely composed of the lawless moss-troopers of the Scotch Border, who looked upon war as a mere excuse for raids, and boasted that everything beyond the Trent was in an enemy's country. Before moving south they harried most thoroughly the estates of the northern Yorkists. Salisbury's patrimony about Middleham and Sherif Hoton bore the brunt of the plunder, at the hands of the retainers of the elder branch of Neville, whose head, Earl Ralph of Westmoreland, put his men under the charge of his brother Thomas, one of the most rabid Lancastrians in the North Country.

About the middle of January the Queen's army began to roll southward, pillaging recklessly on all sides, and sacking from roof to cellar the towns of Grantham, Stamford, Peterborough, Huntingdon, Royston, Melbourn, and Dunstable, as they passed down the Ermine Street.

The news of the battle of Wakefield reached London about January 5th, and set the whole South Country in dismay. Warwick, who had been keeping his Christmas on his own estates, was forced to ride up to the capital at full speed, and assume the direction of affairs, for there was now no one to share the responsibility with him. His uncle, in whose cause he had fought so long, and his father, whose prudent counsels had guided the party, were both gone; his cousin of March, the head of the family, was no more than nineteen years of age, and was moreover at this moment far away by the Severn, looking after the Welsh March. It devolved on Warwick to assume the responsibility for the government of the kingdom and the safety of the Yorkist party.

Though there were traitors enough ready to change to the winning side, as was always the case in this unhappy war, the south-eastern counties were firm to York even in the darkest hour. Warwick found ready assistants in the Duke of Norfolk, the Archbishop of Canterbury, the Earl of Arundel, the Lords Bonville, Cobham, Fitzwalter, and the Commons of Kent and London. "In this country," wrote a partisan of York, "every man is well willing to go with my Lords here, and I hope God shall help them, for the people of the North rob and steal, and are appointed to pillage all this country, and give away men's goods and livelihood in all the South Country, and that shall be a mischief."

To resist the advance of the Queen on London, Warwick marched out to St. Albans and arrayed some thirty thousand men to cover the London road. His army was drawn up not in the great masses which were usual at this time, but in detachments scattered along a front of three miles; the right on a heath called No Man's Land, the left in St. Albans town. The country-side was full of woods and hedges, which were manned by archers, supported by a body of Burgundian handgun-men whom Warwick had hired in Flanders. King Henry was taken along with the army, and stationed in the rear, in charge of Lord Bonville. The position was strong, but the communication between its various parts was bad, and the whole force of Warwick's men seems to have been ill placed for concentration. Owing to some mismanagement of the officer commanding the mounted scouts, the Lancastrians attacked before they were expected. "The Queen's men were at hands with the Earl's in the town of St. Albans while all things were set to seek and out of order, for the prickers came not home to bring tidings that the Queen was at hand, save one, and he came and said that she was yet nine mile off." The first Lancastrian attack on the left, in St. Albans town, was beaten back, but in another part of the field a fatal disaster took place. A Kentish squire named Lovelace, who led a company in the right wing, went over to the enemy, and let the Lancastrians through the Yorkist line. King Henry was captured by his wife's followers "as he sat under a great oak, smiling to see the discomfiture of the army." When the news ran along the front that treachery was at work, and that the King was taken, the bulk of the Yorkists broke up and fled. Not more than three thousand were slain or taken, but the whole force was irretrievably scattered, and the greater part of the leaders fled home to their own lands as if the war was over.

Queen Margaret showed her joy at the recovery of her husband's person by an exhibition of savage cruelty. Lord Bonville and Sir Thomas Kyrriel, who had been in charge of Henry and had been captured with him, were brought before her. "So she told them they must die, and sent for her son the Prince of Wales, and said that he should choose what death they should suffer. And when the boy—he was eight years old—was brought into the tent, she said 'Fair son, what manner of death shall these knights, whom you see here, die?' And the young child answered 'Let them have their heads taken off.' Then said Sir Thomas, 'May God destroy those who taught thee this manner of speech,' but immediately they drew them out and cut off both their heads" (February 17th, 1461).

Chapter 10

TOWTON FIELD

The dispersion of the Yorkist army seems to have been so complete that Warwick could not gather together more than four or five thousand of the thirty thousand men who had stood in line at St. Albans. With this small force he considered himself unable to protect London, and he therefore retreated not southward but westward, intending to fall back on his own Midland estates, to raise fresh troops, and join the Earl of March in the west. He only sent to London to order that his young cousins George and Richard of York—now boys of eleven and nine respectively—should be sent over-sea to take refuge in Flanders.

Accordingly Warwick now marched by vile cross-country roads, and in the worst days of a February which was long remembered for its rains and inundations, across Buckinghamshire and Oxfordshire to Chipping Norton. Here he met with the Earl of March, whose proceedings during the last month require a word of notice.

Edward was at Gloucester when the news of Wakefield reached him, and saw at once that troops must be raised to help Warwick to defend London. Accordingly he moved into the Welsh Marches, and hastily called together some ten or eleven thousand men. With these he would have marched east, if it had not been that Mid Wales had risen in behalf of Queen Margaret, and that he himself was beset by forces headed by Jasper Earl of Pembroke, Jasper's father Owen Tudor, the husband of the Queen Dowager, and James

Earl of Wiltshire. Before he could move to succour Warwick, he must free himself from these adversaries in his rear. The campaign in the West was short and sharp. The Earl of March met the Welsh at Mortimer's Cross, in north Herefordshire near Wigmore, on February 2nd, and gave them a crushing defeat. Owen Tudor was taken prisoner and beheaded, and his head was set on the highest step of the market-cross at Hereford. "And a mad woman combed his hair and washed away the blood from his face, and got candles, and set them about the head burning, more than a hundred, no one hindering her." The Earls of Pembroke and Wiltshire escaped, and joined Queen Margaret with the wrecks of their army.

The moment that he had crushed the Welsh Lancastrians and settled the affairs of the March, Edward had set out for London, hoping to arrive in time to aid Warwick. He could not achieve the impossible, but he had passed the Severn, crossed the bleak Cotswolds, and reached Chipping Norton by February 22nd. Having left some of his troops behind in Wales, he had not more than eight or nine thousand of his Marchmen with him, under Hastings—destined one day to be the victim of Richard of Gloucester—Sir John Wenlock, and William Herbert the future Earl of Pembroke.

The news that reached Warwick and the Earl of March at Chipping Norton was so startling that it caused them to change their whole plan of operations, and to march straight upon London, instead of merely gathering fresh strength to make head in a new campaign in the west Midlands.

The course of events after the fight of St. Albans had been exactly the reverse of what might have been expected from the

Queen's fiery temper and the reckless courage of the Northern bands that followed her.

The battle had been fought upon February 17th, the troops of Warwick had retired westward on the 18th, the victorious army was within thirteen miles of London, and there was nothing to prevent the Queen from entering the city next day. It is one of the most curious problems of English history to find that the Lancastrians lay for eight days quiescent, and made no endeavour to replace the King in his capital. Knowing the extraordinary apathy which the citizens displayed all over England during the Wars of the Roses, we may be sure that the Londoners, in spite of their preference for York, would not have ventured to exclude the Northern army when it claimed admittance at their gates.

But on this one occasion Queen Margaret displayed not only her usual want of judgment, but a want of firmness that was foreign to her character. King Henry, asserting for once some influence on politics, and asserting it to his own harm, had determined to spare London and the home counties the horrors of plunder at the hands of the Northern hordes. Not an armed force but a few envoys were sent to London, while the main body of the troops were held back, and the van pushed no farther than Barnet. Simultaneously the King issued strenuous proclamations against raiding of any kind. This ordinance caused vast murmuring among the Northern Men, observes the Abbot of St. Albans, on whom the King was quartered, but had not the least effect in curbing their propensity to plunder.

The Londoners had quite made up their minds to submit; their only thought was to buy their pardon as cheaply as possible at the

King's hands. On the 20th they sent the Duchesses of Bedford and Buckingham—the widows of the great Regent of France and of the Lancastrian Duke slain at Northampton—together with certain aldermen, to plead for grace and peace at the hands of the Queen. The King and Queen were found at Barnet, whither they had moved from St. Albans, and gave not unpropitious answers, although that very morning Margaret had doomed to execution the unfortunate Bonville and Kyrriel. As a proof of their good intentions they undertook to move back their army out of reach of the city; accordingly on Thursday the 25th the Northerners, in a state of deep disgust, were sent back to Dunstable.

The first demand which the Queen had made on London was for a supply of provisions for her army; and on Friday the 26th the Mayor and aldermen gathered a long train of waggons, laden with "all sorts of victuals, and much Lenten stuff," and prepared to despatch it northward. The city, however, was in a great state of disturbance. Public feeling was excited by the plundering of the Lancastrians, and news had arrived that the cause of York was not lost, and that a Yorkist army was marching to the relief of London. To the horror of the more prudent citizens, a mob, headed by Sir John Wenlock's cook, stopped the carts at Newgate, plundered the provisions, and drove the waggoners away.

Such an act was bound to draw down punishment, and that same afternoon a great body of Lancastrian men-at-arms, under Sir Baldwin Fulford, was pushed up to Westminster to overawe the city. The Londoners had to make up their minds that Friday evening whether they would fight or submit, and many were the heart-searchings of the timid aldermen; but on Saturday morning their grief was turned into joy. News arrived that Warwick and the Earl of March were at hand: Fulford's men abandoned Westminster and fell back northward; and ere the day was out the travel-stained troops of the Yorkist lords were defiling into the city. By nightfall ten thousand men were within the gates, and all thought of surrender was gone.

Thus King Henry's good intentions and Queen Margaret's unexpected irresolution had lost London to the Lancastrians. But their army still lay in a threatening attitude at Dunstable, and it seemed inevitable that the Earl of March would have either to fight a battle or to stand a siege before he was a week older.

But before the fate of England was put to the arbitrament of combat there was one thing to be done. The cruel deaths of York and Salisbury had driven the quarrel between York and Lancaster beyond the possibility of accommodation. In spite of all the personal respect that was felt for King Henry, it was no longer possible that the heir of Duke Richard should be content to pose merely as the destined successor to the throne. Now that Henry was again in the hands of his wife and the Beauforts, it was certain that the royal name would be used to the utmost against the Yorkists. They must have some cry to set against the appeal to national loyalty which would be made in the name of King Henry.

No doubt Warwick and Edward had settled the whole matter on their ride from Chipping Norton to London, for their action showed every sign of having been long planned out. On the Sunday morning, within twenty-four hours of their arrival in the city, their army was drawn out "in the great field outside Clerkenwell," and while a great multitude of Londoners stood by,

George Bishop of Exeter, the orator of the Neville clan, made a solemn statement of Edward's claim to the throne. At once soldiers and citizens joined in the shout, "God save King Edward!" and there was no doubt of the spontaneity of their enthusiasm. The heart of the people was with York, and it only remained necessary to legalise their choice by some form of election.

Save the three Nevilles, Warwick, Fauconbridge, and Bishop George, there seems to have been no peer with Edward at the moment. Warwick felt that it would not look well that his cousin should ostensibly receive his crown from the Nevilles alone, whatever might be the reality of the case. Accordingly the few Yorkist peers within reach were hastily summoned. The Archbishop of Canterbury came in from Kent, where he had been "waiting for better times." The Duke of Norfolk, Lord Fitzwalter, Lord Ferrers of Chartley, and the Bishop of Salisbury appeared ere two days were out. Then these eight peers, spiritual and temporal, with a dozen or so of knights, and a deputation of London citizens, solemnly met at Baynard's Castle and declared Edward King. There had not been an instance of the election of a monarch by such a scanty body of supporters since the meeting of the Witan that chose Henry the First. The house of Neville and their cousin of Norfolk were practically the sole movers in the business.

Next day, Thursday March 4th, Edward rode in state to Westminster with his scanty following of notables. There before the high altar he declared his title, and sat on his throne, with the sceptre of Edward the Confessor in his hand, beneath a canopy, receiving the homage and fealty of his adherents. Then embarking in a state barge he returned by water to the Tower where he fixed his abode, deserting the York family mansion of Baynard's Castle. Meanwhile the heralds proclaimed him at every street corner as Edward the Fourth, King of France and England, and Lord of Ireland.

Every one had been expecting that the coronation would be interrupted by the news that Queen Margaret's army was thundering at the gates; but no signs of the approach of an enemy appeared, and that same day it was known that the Queen had broken up from Dunstable and marched away northward. Her troops were in a state of incipient disbandment: they had refused to obey the King's proclamation against plunder, and had melted away by thousands, some to harry the Home Counties, some to bear off booty already obtained. The men that still adhered to the standards were so few and so discontented that the Lancastrian lords begged the Queen to retreat. They had heard exaggerated rumours of the strength of King Edward, and dared not fight him. Accordingly Henry, his wife and son, and his nobles, with their whole following, rode off along the Watling Street, sending before them messengers to raise the whole force of the North, and to bid it meet their retiring army on the borders of Yorkshire.

The festivities of the coronation had not prevented the Yorkist lords from keeping the imminence of their danger close before their eyes. The ceremony had taken place on Thursday afternoon; by early dawn on Friday Mowbray had ridden off eastward to array his followers in Norfolk and Suffolk. On the Saturday Warwick himself marched out by the great North road, with the war-tried troops who had fought under him at St. Albans and accompanied his retreat to Chipping Norton. He moved on cautiously, gathering in the Yorkist knights of the Midlands and his own Warwickshire and Worcestershire retainers, till he had been joined by the whole force of his party. For four or five days after Warwick had set forth, the levies of the Southern Counties continued to pour into London. On the 10th the main body of infantry marched on to unite with the Earl; they were some fifteen thousand strong, Marchmen from the Welsh Border and Kentishmen; for Kent, ever loyal to York, had turned out its archers in full force, under a notable captain named Robert Horne. Finally, King Edward—who had remained behind till the last available moment, cheering the Londoners, bidding for the support of doubtful adherents, getting together money, and signing the manifold documents which had to be drawn up on his accession—started with his personal following, amid the cheers of the citizens and cries for vengeance on King Henry and his wife.

Warwick had pushed forward cautiously, keeping in his front some light horse under John Ratcliff, who claimed the barony of Fitzwalter. King Edward, on the other hand, came on at full speed, and was able to over-take his vanguard at Leicester. Mowbray, with the troops from the Eastern Counties, was less ready; he was several days behind the King, and, as we shall see, did not come up till the actual eve of battle.

There had been some expectation that the Lancastrians would fight on the line of the Trent, for the Northern lords tarried some days at Nottingham. But as Warwick pushed on he had always found the enemy retreating before him. Their route could be traced by the blazing villages on each side of their path, for the Northern men had gone homewards excited to bitter wrath by the loss of the plunder of London. They had eaten up the whole country-side, swept off the horses, pulled the very houses to pieces in search of hidden goods, stripped every man, woman, and child they met of purse and raiment, even to the beggars who came out to ask them for charity, and slain every man that raised a hand against them. Beyond the Trent, they said, they were in an enemy's country. In the eyes of every Southern man the measure of their iniquities was full.

When Warwick and King Edward learnt that the Queen and the Northern lords had drawn their plundering bands north of the Trent, they had not much difficulty in settling the direction of their march. It was practically certain that the Lancastrians would be found on one of the positions across the Great North Road which cover the approach to York. Now, as in every age since the Romans built their great line of communication between north and south, it would be on the line between York and Lincoln that the fate of Northern England would be decided. The only doubt was whether the Lancastrians would choose to defend the Don or the Aire or the Wharfe, behind each of which they might take up their position.

On the Friday, March 26th, the Yorkists crossed the Don unmolested, but the news was not long in reaching them that the enemy lay behind the next obstacle, the Aire, now swollen to a formidable torrent by the spring rains, and likely to cause much trouble ere it could be crossed. King Henry with his wife and son lay at York, but all his lords with their retainers lay in the villages about Tadcaster and Cawood midway between the Wharfe and

Aire, with their central camp hard by the church of Towton, which was destined to give its name to the coming battle.

To secure the passage of the Aire was now the task that was incumbent on the Yorkists. Accordingly their vanguard under Lord Fitzwalter was sent forward in haste on to Ferrybridge, where the Roman road crosses the stream. Contrary to expectation the place was found unoccupied, and its all-important bridge secured. The line of the Aire was won; but the Friday was not destined to pass without bloodshed. The Northern lords, cursing the carelessness which had lost them their line of defence, determined to fall on the advanced guard of the enemy, and beat it out of Ferrybridge before the main body should come up. Lord Clifford, who commanded the nearest detachment, rode off at once from Towton, and charged into Ferrybridge while the newly-arrived Yorkists were at their meal. Fitzwalter had kept as careless a watch as his enemies; he was taken unprepared, his men were routed, and he himself slain as he tried to rally them. At nightfall Clifford held the town, and slept there undisturbed.

Next morning, however, the situation was changed. Somerset, or rather the council of the Lancastrian lords, had taken no measures to support Clifford. He was left alone at Ferrybridge with the few thousand men of his original force, while the main army was slowly gathering on Towton hill-side eight miles to the rear. Meanwhile the Yorkist main body was approaching Ferrybridge from the south, and a detached column under Lord Fauconbridge, stoutest of Warwick's many uncles, was trying the dangerous passage at Castleford, three miles away, where there was no one to resist them. Hearing that Fauconbridge was already across, and was moving round to cut him off from his base, Clifford evacuated Ferrybridge and fell back towards his main body. He had already accomplished six of the eight miles of his journey, when near Dintingdale Fauconbridge suddenly came in upon his flank with a very superior force. Clifford had so nearly reached his friends that he was marching in perfect security. The Yorkists scattered his men before they could form up to fight, and killed him ere he had even time to brace on his helmet. The survivors of his detachment were chased in upon the Lancastrian main army, which was so badly served by its scouts that it had neither heard of Fauconbridge's approach nor taken any measures to bring in Clifford's party in safety. Nay, so inert were the Lancastrian commanders, that they did not, after the skirmish, march out to beat off Fauconbridge, whose friends were still miles away, painfully threading the bridge of Ferrybridge or the ford at Castleford.

All through Saturday the Yorkists were slowly coming up to reinforce their vanguard, but the roads and the weather were so bad that the rear was still on the other side of the Aire when night fell. However, the main body was safely concentrated on a ridge south of Saxton village, and probably thirty-five thousand out of Edward's forty-eight thousand men were in line, though much famished for victuals. The belated rear-guard, which was destined to form the right wing of the army on the morrow, was composed of the troops from the Eastern Counties under Mowbray; with him were Sir John Wenlock and Sir John Dynham, two of Warwick's most trusted friends. They were not expected to come up till some hours after daybreak on Sunday morning. With the Yorkist main body were the King, Warwick, his brother John, his uncle Fauconbridge, Lord Scrope, Lord Berners, Lord Stanley, Sir William Hastings, Sir John Stafford, Sir Walter Blunt, Robert Horne, the leader of the Kentishmen, and many other South-Country knights and squires.

Two miles north of the Yorkist camp at Saxton, the Lancastrians lay in full force on Towton hill-side. They had with them the largest army that was ever put into the field during the whole war. Somerset, Exeter, James Butler the Irish Earl who had endeavoured to rival Warwick's power in Wiltshire, Courtney Earl of Devon, Moleyns, Hungerford, and Willoughby had brought in the South-Country adherents of Lancaster, those at least of them whom the fields of St. Albans and Northampton had left unharmed and unabashed. Sir Andrew Trollope was there, with the remnant of the trained troops from Calais who had deserted York at Ludford in the previous year. But the bulk of the sixty thousand men who served under the Red Rose were the retainers of the Northern lords. Henry Percy of Northumberland appeared in person with all his following. The Durham vassals of the elder house of Neville were arrayed under John Lord Neville, the younger brother of Ralph of Westmoreland, though the Earl himself was (now as always) not forthcoming in person. Beside the Neville and Percy retainers were the bands of Lords Dacre, Welles, Roos, Beaumont, Mauley, and of the dead Clifford—of all the barons and knights indeed of the North Country save of the younger house of Neville.

The Lancastrian position was very strong. Eight miles north of Ferrybridge the Great North Road is flanked by a long plateau some hundred and fifty feet above the level of the surrounding country, the first rising ground to the west that breaks the plain of York. The high road to Tadcaster creeps along its eastern foot, and then winds round its northern extremity; its western side is skirted by a brook called the Cock, which was then in flood and only passable at a few points beside the bridge where the high road crosses it. The Lancastrians were drawn up across the plateau, their left wing on the high road, their right touching the steep bank of the Cock. One flank was completely covered by the flooded stream, while the other, the one which lay over the road, could only be turned by the enemy if he went down into the plain and exposed himself to a flank attack while executing his movement. The ground, however, was very cramped for an army of sixty thousand men; it was less than a mile and a half in breadth, and it seems likely that the Lancastrians must, contrary to the usual English custom, have formed several lines, one in rear of the other, in order to crowd their men on to such a narrow space.

The Yorkists at Saxton lay just on the southern declivity of the plateau, within two miles of the Lancastrian line of battle, whose general disposition must have been rendered sufficiently evident by the countless watchfires along the rising ground.

Although they knew themselves to be outnumbered by the enemy, Warwick and King Edward were determined to attack. Each of them had a father to revenge, and they were not disposed to count heads. Before it was dawn, at four o'clock on the morning of that eventful Palm Sunday, the Yorkist army was drawn out. The King rode down the line bidding them remember that they had the just cause, and the men began to climb the gentle ascent of the

Towton plateau. The left wing, which was slightly in advance of the main body, was led by Fauconbridge; the great central mass by Warwick in person; the King was in command of the reserve. Of the details of the marshalling we know no more, but the Yorkist line, though only thirty-five thousand strong, was drawn up on a front equal to that which the sixty thousand Lancastrians occupied, and must therefore have been much thinner. When Norfolk and the missing right wing should appear, it was obvious that they would outflank the enemy on the side of the plain. Warwick's plan, therefore, was evidently to engage the Lancastrians so closely and so occupy their attention that Norfolk should be able to take them in flank without molestation on his arrival.

In the dusk of the March morning, with a strong north wind blowing in their faces, the clumps of Yorkist billmen and archers commenced to mount the hill. No opposition was made to their approach, but when they had advanced for one thousand yards along the summit of the plateau, they dimly descried the Lancastrian host in order of battle, on the farther side of a slight dip in the ground called Towtondale. At the same moment the wind veered round, and a heavy fall of snow commenced to beat in the faces of the Lancastrians. So thick was it that the two armies could only make out each other's position from the simultaneous shout of defiance which ran down each line. Fauconbridge, whose wing lay nearest to the enemy, determined to utilise the accident of the snow in a manner which throws the greatest credit on his presence of mind. He sent forward his archers to the edge of the dip in the plateau, with orders to discharge a few flights of arrows into the Lancastrian columns, and then to retire back again to the line of battle. This they did; the wind bore their arrows into the crowded masses, who with the snow beating into their eyes could not see the enemy that was molesting them, and considerable execution was done. Accordingly the whole Lancastrian line of archers commenced to reply; but as they were shooting against the wind, and as Fauconbridge's men had withdrawn after delivering their volley, it resulted that the Northeners continued to pour a heavy flight of arrows into the unoccupied ground forty yards in front of the Yorkist position. Their fire was so fast and furious that ere very long their shafts began to run short. When this became noticeable, Fauconbridge led his men forward again to the edge of Towtondale, and recommenced his deadly volleys into the enemy's right wing. The Lancastrians could make little or no reply, their store of missiles being almost used up; their position was growing unbearable, and with a simultaneous impulse the whole mass facing Fauconbridge plunged down into Towtondale, to cross the dip and fall on the enemy at close quarters. The movement spread down the line from west to east, and in a few minutes the two armies were engaged along their whole front. Thus the Lancastrians, though fighting on their own chosen ground, had to become the assailants, and were forced to incur the disadvantage of having the slope against them, as they struggled up the southern side of the declivity of Towtondale.

Of all the battles of the Wars of the Roses, perhaps indeed of all the battles in English history, the fight of Towton was the most desperate and the most bloody. For sheer hard fighting there is nothing that can compare to it; from five in the morning to mid-day the battle never slackened for a moment. No one ever again complained that the Southern men were less tough than the Northern. Time after time the Lancastrians rolled up the southern slope of Towtondale and flung themselves on the Yorkist host; sometimes they were driven down at once, sometimes they pushed the enemy back for a space, but they could never break the King's line. Each time that an attacking column was repelled, newly-rallied troops took its place, and the push of pike never ceased. We catch one glimpse of Warwick in the midst of the tumult. Waurin tells how "the greatest press of the battle lay on the quarter where the Earl of Warwick stood," and Whethamsted describes him "pressing on like a second Hector, and encouraging his young soldiers;" but there is little to be gathered about the details of the fight.[5] There cannot have been much to learn, for each combatant, lost in the mist and drifting snow, could tell only of what was going on in his own immediate neighbourhood. They have only left us vague pictures of horror, "the dead hindered the living from coming to close quarters, they lay so thick," "there was more red than white visible on the snow," are the significant remarks of the chronicler. King Henry, as he heard his Palm-Sunday mass in York Minster ten miles away—"he was kept off the field because he was better at praying than at fighting," says the Yorkist chronicler—may well have redoubled his prayers, for never was there to be such a slaughter of Englishmen.

At length the object for which Warwick's stubborn billmen had so long maintained their ground against such odds was attained. The column under the Duke of Norfolk, which was to form the Yorkist right wing, began to come up from Ferrybridge. Its route brought it out on the extreme left flank of the Lancastrians, where the high road skirts the plateau. Too heavily engaged in front to suspect that all the army of York was not yet before them, Somerset and his colleagues had made no provision against a new force appearing beyond their left wing. Thus Norfolk's advancing columns were able to turn the exposed flank, open an enfilading fire upon the enemy's left rear, and, what was still more important, to cut him off from all lines of retreat save that which led across the flooded Cock. The effect of Norfolk's advance was at once manifest; the battle began to roll northward and westward, as the Lancastrians gave back and tried to form a new front against the unsuspected enemy. But the moment that they began to retire the whole Yorkist line followed them. The arrival of Norfolk had been to Warwick's men what the arrival of Blücher was to Wellington's at Waterloo; after having fought all the day on the defensive they had their opportunity at last, and were eager to use it. When the Lancastrians had once begun to retire they found themselves so hotly pushed on that they could never form a new line of battle. Their gross numbers were crushed more and more closely together as the pressure on their left flank became more and more marked, and if any reserves yet remained in hand, there was no way of bringing them to the front. Yet, as all the chroniclers acknowledge, the Northern men gave way to no panic; they turned again and again, and strove to dispute every step between Towtondale and the edge of the plateau. It took three hours more of fighting to roll them off the rising ground; but when once they were driven down their position became terrible. The Cock when in flood is in many places unfordable; sometimes it spreads out so as to cover the fields for fifty yards on each side of its wonted bed; and the only safe retreat across it was by the single bridge on the Tadcaster road. The sole result of the desperate fighting of the Lancastrians was that this deadly obstacle now lay in their immediate rear. The whole mass was compelled to pass the river as best it could. Some escaped by the bridge; many forded the Cock where its stream ran shallow; many yielded themselves as prisoners—some to get quarter, others not, for the Yorkists were wild with the rage of ten hours' slaughter. But many thousands had a worse fortune; striving to ford the river where it was out of their depth, or trodden down in the shallower parts by their own flying comrades, they died without being touched by the Yorkist steel. Any knight or man-at-arms who lost his footing in the water was doomed, for the cumbrous armour of the later fifteenth century made it quite impossible to rise again. Even the billman and archer in his salet and jack would find it hard to regain his feet. Hence we may well believe the chroniclers when they tell us that the Cock slew its thousands that day, and that the last Lancastrians who crossed its waters crossed them on a bridge composed of the bodies of their comrades.

Even this ghastly scene was not to be the end of the slaughter; the Yorkists urged the pursuit for miles from the field, nearly to the gates of York, still slaying as they went. The hapless King Henry, with his wife and son, were borne out of the town by their flying followers, who warned them that the enemy was still close behind, and were fain to take the road for Durham and the Border. Only Richard Tunstal, the King's Chamberlain, and five horsemen more guarded them during the flight.

When Warwick and King Edward drew in their men from the pursuit, and bade the heralds count the slain, they must have felt that their fathers were well avenged. Nearly thirty thousand corpses lay on the trampled snow of the plateau, or blocked the muddy course of the Cock, or strewed the road to Tadcaster and York; and of these only eight thousand were Yorkists. The sword had fallen heavily on the Lancastrian leaders. The Earl of Northumberland was carried off by his followers mortally wounded, and died next day. Of the barons, Dacre, Neville, Mauley, and Welles, lay on the field. Thomas Courtney the Earl of Devon was taken alive—a worse fate than that of his fellows, for the headsman's axe awaited him. Of leaders below the baronial rank there were slain Sir Andrew Trollope, the late Lieutenant of Calais, Sir Ralph Grey, Sir Henry Beckingham, and many more whom it would be tedious to name. The slaughter had been as deadly to the Northern knighthood as was Flodden a generation later to the noble houses of Scotland; there was hardly a family that had not to mourn the loss of its head or heir.

The uphill fight which the Yorkists had to wage during the earlier hours of the day had left its mark in their ranks; eight thousand had fallen, one man for every six in the field. But the leaders had come off fortunately; only Sir John Stafford and Robert Horne, the Kentish captain, had fallen. So long indeed as the fight ran level, the knights in their armour of proof were comparatively safe; it was always the pursuit which proved so fatal to the chiefs of a broken army.

Footnotes

5. There is nothing authentic to be discovered of the story mentioned by Monstrelet, and popularised in Warwickshire tradition, that the Earl slew his charger at Towton to show his men that he would not fly.

Chapter 11

THE TRIUMPH OF KING EDWARD

On the evening of that bloody Palm Sunday, King Edward, Warwick, and the other Yorkist chiefs, slept in the villages round the battlefield. Next morning, however, they set their weary army on the march to reap the fruits of victory. In the afternoon they appeared before the gates of York, where the heads of York and Salisbury, bleached with three months of winter rains, still looked southward from the battlements. The citizens had, as was usual in the time, not the slightest intention of offering resistance, but they must have felt many a qualm as Edward's men, drunk with slaughter and set on revenging the harrying of the South by the Queen's army, drew up before their walls.

Edward, however, had already fixed on the policy from which he never swerved throughout his reign—hard measure for the great and easy measure for the small. The Mayor and citizens were allowed to "find means of grace through Lord Berners and Sir John Neville, brother to the Earl of Warwick"—doubtless through a sufficient gift of rose nobles. These two lords led the Mayor and Council before the King, who promptly granted them grace, and was then received into the town "with great solemnity and processions." There Edward kept his Easter week, and made every arrangement for the subjugation of the North. His first act was to take down the heads of his father and his uncle from over the gate, and provide for their reverent burial. His next was to mete out to his Lancastrian prisoners the measure that York and Salisbury had received. The chief of them, Courtney Earl of Devon and the Bastard of Exeter, were decapitated in the market-place, and their heads sent south to be set up on London Bridge. James Earl of Wiltshire—long Salisbury's rival in the South—was caught a few days later, and suffered the same fate.

The submission of the various Yorkshire towns was not long in coming in, and it was soon ascertained that no further resistance was to be looked for south of the Tees. The broken bands of the Lancastrians had disappeared from Yorkshire, and Warwick's tenants from Middleham and Sherif Hoton were now able to come in to explain to their lord how they had fared during the Lancastrian ascendency at the hands of his cousins of Westmoreland. In common with the few other Yorkists of the North, they had received hard measure; they had been well plundered, and probably constrained to pay up all that the Westmorelands could wring out of them, as arrears for the twenty years during which the Yorkshire lands of Neville had been out of the hands of the senior branch.

A few days after Easter, Warwick and Edward moved out of York and pushed on to Durham. On the way they were entertained at Middleham with such cheer as the place could afford after its plunder by the Lancastrians. Nowhere did they meet with any resistance, and the task of finishing the war appeared so simple that the King betook himself homeward about May 1st, leaving Warwick with a general commission to pacify the North. John Neville remained behind with his brother, as did Sir Robert Ogle and Sir John Coniers, the only two Yorkists of importance in the North outside the Neville family. The King took with him the rest of the lords, who were wanted for the approaching festivals and councils in London, and with them the bulk of the army.

The task which Warwick had received turned out to be a much more formidable matter than had been expected. King Henry, Queen Margaret, the Dukes of Somerset and Exeter, Lords Hungerford and Roos, with the other surviving Lancastrian leaders, had fled to Scotland, where they had succeeded in inducing the Scotch regents—Kennedy, Boyd, and their fellows—to continue the policy of the late King, and throw themselves heartily into the war with the Yorkists. The inducement offered was the cession of Berwick and Carlisle, and the former town was at once handed over "and well stuffed with Scots." Nor was it only on Scotch aid that the Lancastrians relied; they had determined to make application to the King of France, and Somerset and Hungerford sailed for the Continent at the earliest opportunity. They were stayed at Dieppe by orders of the wily Louis the Eleventh, who was averse to committing himself to either party in the English struggle while his own crown was hardly three months old; but their mission was not to be without its results. Putting aside the hope of assistance from France and Scotland, the Lancastrians had still some resources of their own on which they might count. A few scattered bands of Percy retainers still kept the field in Northumberland, and the Percy crescent still floated over the strong castles of Alnwick, Bamborough, and Dunstanburgh.

The problem which fell into Warwick's hands was to clear the routed Lancastrians out of Northumberland, and at the same time to keep good watch against the inroads of the Scotch and the English refugees who were leagued with them. Defensive and offensive operations would have to be combined, for, on the one hand, the siege of the Percy castles must be formed—and sieges in the fifteenth century were slow and weary work—while, on the other, the raids of the lords of the Scotch Border might occur at any time and place, and had to be met without delay. Warwick was forced to divide his troops, undertaking himself to cover the line of the Tyne and observe the Northumbrian castles, while his brother John, who for his services at Towton had just been created Lord Montagu, took charge of the force which was to fend off Scotch attacks on the Western Marches.

In June the Scots and the English refugees crossed the Border in force; their main body made a push to seize Carlisle, which the Lancastrian chiefs, the Duke of Exeter and Lord Grey de Rougemont, promised to deliver to them as they had already delivered Berwick. The town, however, shut its gates; and the invaders were constrained to content themselves with burning its suburbs and forming a regular siege. But as they lay before it they were suddenly attacked by Montagu, who came up long before he was expected, and beat them back over the Border with the loss of several thousand men; among the slain was John Clifford, brother to the peer who had fallen at Towton.

Almost simultaneously another raiding party, led by Lord Roos and Sir John Fortescu, the late Chief-Justice, and guided by two of the Westmoreland Nevilles, Thomas and Humphrey, slipped down from the Middle Marches and attempted to raise the county of Durham. But as they drew near to the ancestral Neville seat of Brancepeth, they were fallen upon by forces brought up by

Warwick, and were driven back on June 26th as disastrously as the main army for which they had been making a diversion.

These two defeats cooled the ardour of the Scotch allies of the house of Lancaster. Moreover, trouble was soon provided for them on their own side of the Border. There were always discontented nobles to be found in the North, and King Edward was able to retaliate on the Scotch regents by concluding a treaty with the Earl of Ross, which set a considerable rebellion on foot in the Highlands and the Western Isles. By the time that the autumn came there was no longer any immediate danger to be apprehended on the Borders, and Warwick was able to relinquish his northern viceroyalty and come south, to pay his estates a flying visit, and to obey the writ which summoned him in November to King Edward's first Parliament at Westminster.

While Warwick had been labouring in the North, the King had been holding his Court at London, free to rule after his own devices. At twenty Edward the Fourth had already a formed character, and displayed all the personal traits which developed in his later years. The spirit of the fifteenth century was strong in him. Cultured and cruel, as skilled as the oldest statesman in the art of cajoling the people, as cool in the hour of danger as the oldest soldier, he was not a sovereign with whom even the greatest of his subjects could deal lightly. Yet he was so inordinately fond of display and luxury of all sorts, so given to sudden fits of idleness, so prone to sacrifice policy to any whim or selfish impulse of the moment, that he must have seemed at times almost contemptible to a man who, like Warwick, had none of the softer vices of self-indulgence. Still in mourning for a father and brother not six months dead, with a kingdom not yet fully subdued to his fealty, with an empty exchequer, with half the nobles and gentry of England owing him a blood-feud for their kinsmen slain at Towton, Edward had cast aside every thought of the past and the morrow, and was bearing himself with all the thriftless good-humour of an heir lately come to a well-established fortune. It seems that the splendours of his coronation-feasts were the main things that had been occupying his mind while Warwick had been fighting his battles in the North. Reading of his jousts and banquets and processions, his gorgeous reception by the city magnates, and his lavish distributions of honours and titles, we hardly remember that he was no firmly-rooted King, but the precarious sovereign of a party, surrounded by armed enemies and secret conspirators.

In the lists of honours which Edward had distributed after his return homeward from Towton field, Warwick found that he had not been neglected. The offices which he had held in 1458-59 had been restored to him; he was again Captain of the town and castle of Calais, Lieutenant of the March of Picardy, Grand Chamberlain of England, and High Steward of the Duchy of Lancaster. In addition he was now created Constable of Dover and Warden of the Cinque Ports, and made Master of the Mews and Falcons, and Steward of the Manor and Forest of Feckenham. His position in the North, too, was made regular by his appointment as Warden and Commissary General of the East and West Marches, and Procurator Envoy and Deputy for all negotiations with the Scots.

Nor had the rest of the Neville clan been overlooked. John Neville had, as we have already mentioned, received the barony of Montagu. George Neville the Bishop of Exeter was again

Chancellor. Fauconbridge, who had fought so manfully at Towton, was created Earl of Kent. Moreover, Sir John Wenlock, Warwick's most faithful adherent, who had done him such good service at Sandwich in 1459, was made a baron. We shall always find him true to the cause of his patron down to his death at Tewkesbury field. Although several other creations swelled the depleted ranks of the peerage at the same time, the Nevilles could not complain that they had failed to receive their due share of the rewards.

Nor would it seem that at first the King made any effort to resent the natural ascendency which his cousin exercised over his counsels. The experienced warrior of thirty-three must still have overborne the precocious lad of twenty when their wills came into contact. The campaigns of 1459-60, in which he had learnt soldiering under Warwick, must have long remained impressed on Edward's mind, even after he had won his own laurels at Mortimer's Cross and shared with equal honours in the bloody triumph of Towton. So long as Richard Neville was still in close and constant contact with the young King, his ascendency was likely to continue. It was when, in the succeeding years, his duties took him for long periods far from Edward's side, that the Earl was to find his cousin first growing indifferent, then setting his own will against his adviser's, then deliberately going to work to override every scheme that came to him from any member of the Neville house.

We have no particular notice of Warwick's personal doings in the Parliament which sat in November and December 1461; but the language of his brother George the Chancellor represents, no doubt, the attitude which the whole family adopted. His text was

"Amend your ways and your doings," and the tenor of his discourse was to point out that the ills of England during the last generation came from the national apostasy in having deserted the rightful heirs so long in behalf of the usurping house of Lancaster. Now that a new reign had commenced, a reform in national morality should accompany the return of the English to their lawful allegiance. The sweeping acts of attainder against fourteen peers and many scores of knights and squires which the Yorkist Parliament passed might not seem a very propitious beginning for the new era, but at any rate it should be remembered to the credit of the Nevilles that the King's Council under their guidance tempered the zeal of the Commons by many limitations which guarded the rights of numerous individuals who would have been injured by the original proposals.

Moreover, the Government allowed the opportunity of reconciliation to many of the more luke-warm adherents of Lancaster, who had not been personally engaged in the last struggle. It is to Warwick's credit that his cousin Ralph of Westmoreland was admitted to pardon, and not taken to task for the doings of his retainers, under the conduct of his brother, in the campaign of Wakefield and St. Albans. Ralph was summoned to the Parliament, and treated no worse than if he had been a consistent adherent of York. The same favour was granted to the Earl of Oxford, till he forfeited it by deliberate conspiracy against the King. Sanguine men were already beginning to hope that King Edward and his advisers might be induced to end the civil wars by a general grant of amnesty, and might invite his rival Henry to return to England as the first subject of the Crown. Such mercy and reconciliation, however, were beyond the mind of the ordinary partisan of York; and the popular feeling of the day was probably on the side of the correspondent of the Pastons, who complained "that the King receives such men as have been his great enemies, and great oppressors of his Commons, while such as have assisted his Highness be not rewarded; which is to be considered, or else it will hurt, as seemeth me but reason."

Charles W. Oman

Chapter 12

THE PACIFICATION OF THE NORTH

Whatever the partisans of peace may have hoped in the winter of 1461-62, there was in reality no prospect of a general pacification so long as the indomitable Margaret of Anjou was still at liberty and free to plot against the quiet of England. The defeats of her Scotch allies in the summer of 1461 had only spurred her to fresh exertions. In the winter, while Edward's Parliament was sitting at Westminster, she was busy hatching a new scheme for simultaneous risings in various parts of England, accompanied by descents from France and Brittany aided by a Castilian fleet. Somerset and Hungerford had got some countenance from the King of France, and Margaret's own hopeful heart built on this small foundation a great scheme for the invasion of England. A Scotch raid, a rising in Wales, a descent of Bretons upon Guernsey and Jersey, and a great French landing at Sandwich, were to synchronise: "if weather and wind had served them, they should have had one hundred and twenty thousand men on foot in England upon Candlemass Day." But weather and wind were unpropitious, and the only tangible result of the plan was to cost the life of the Earl of Oxford, who had been told off to head the insurgents of the Eastern Counties. He had been taken into favour by King Edward, and we need have small pity for him when he was detected in correspondence with the Queen at the very time that he was experiencing the clemency of her rival. But it was an evil sign of the times that he and his son were executed, not after a regular trial before their peers, but by a special and unconstitutional court held by the Earl of Worcester as Constable of England. For this evil precedent Warwick must take the blame no less than Edward.

But Margaret of Anjou had not yet exhausted her energy. So soon as the storms of winter were over and Somerset returned from France without the promised succours, she resolved to set out in person to stimulate the zeal of Louis the Eleventh, and to gather help from her various relatives on the Continent. Escaping from Scotland by the Irish Sea, she rounded the Land's End and came ashore with her young son in Brittany. The Duke gave her twelve thousand crowns, and passed her on to her father Réné in Anjou. From his Court she went on to King Louis, who lay at Rouen. With him she had more success than might have been expected, though far less of course than she had hoped. Louis was able to show that he had already got together a fleet, reinforced by some Breton and Castilian vessels, in the mouth of the Seine. In return for an agreement by which Margaret promised the cession of Calais, and perhaps that of the Channel Isles, he undertook to engage frankly in the war, and to put at Margaret's disposition a force for the invasion of England. The way in which Louis chose a leader for this army was very characteristic of the man. He had in close confinement at the time a favourite of his father and an enemy of his own, Peter de Brézé, Count of Maulévrier and Seneschal of Normandy. De Brézé was a gallant knight and a skilled leader; only a few years before he had distinguished himself in the English war, and among other achievements had taken and sacked Sandwich. The King now offered him the choice of staying in prison or of taking charge of an expedition to Scotland in aid of Margaret. De Brézé accepted with alacrity the latter alternative, as much, we are told, from chivalrous desire to assist a distressed Queen as from dislike for the inside of the dungeons of Loches. Quite satisfied, apparently, at getting an enemy out of the country on a dangerous quest, Louis gave him twenty thousand livres in money, forty small vessels, and about two thousand men, and bade him take the Queen whither she would go.

While Louis and Margaret were negotiating, their English enemies had been acting with their accustomed vigour. When May came round Warwick again resumed command of the Northern Border, and marched out to finish the work that had been begun in the previous year. He was already on Scottish ground, and had taken at least one castle north of the Border, when he received a herald from the Scotch regents offering to treat for peace. By his commission, drawn up in the last year, Warwick was authorised to act as plenipotentiary in any such matter. Accordingly he sent back his army and went himself to Dumfries, where he met Mary, the Dowager Queen of Scotland, and the majority of the regents. They concluded an armistice to last till St. Bartholomew's Day, and then set to work to discuss terms of peace. The common report ran that the Scots were ready not only to give up the Lancastrian cause, but even to deliver over the person of King Henry. Moreover, there was talk of an alliance by marriage between the English King and a Scotch Princess. This new departure, mainly brought about by the Queen-Dowager's influence,[6] was not without its effect on the Lancastrian partisans, who found themselves left unsupported to resist Warwick's army, which was, during the negotiations, put under the command of his brother Montagu and set to reduce the Northumbrian fortresses. King Henry fled from the Scotch Court and took refuge in one of the castles of the Archbishop of St. Andrews, the chief member of the regency who opposed peace with England. Lord Dacre, brother of the peer who fell at Towton, surrendered himself to Montagu, and was sent to London, where King Edward received him into grace. Even Somerset himself, the chief of the party, lost heart, and began to send secret letters to Warwick to ascertain whether there was any hope of pardon for him. Meanwhile Naworth Castle was surrendered to Montagu, and the more important stronghold of Alnwick yielded itself to Lord Hastings, who had been detached to form its siege. Bamborough was given up by Sir William Tunstal, and of all the Northern fortresses only Dunstanburgh remained in Lancastrian hands, and it seemed that this place must fall ere the year was out.

Believing that the war was practically at an end, Warwick now turned south, and rode up to London to lay the Scotch proposal before the King. But he had not long left the Border when the whole aspect of affairs was once more transformed by the reappearance of Queen Margaret on the scene.

While Montagu and Warwick had been in the North, King Edward had been sorely vexed by rumours of French invasion. Seventy French and Spanish ships were roaming the Channel, and Fauconbridge, who had set out to find them with a hastily-raised fleet, came home without success. A French force had mustered in Picardy, and Queen Margaret lay all the summer at Boulogne, tampering with the garrison of Calais, who had fallen into mutiny on account of long arrears of pay. But Calais failed to revolt, Louis made no serious attempt on England, and the Queen at last grew impatient and determined to start herself for England, though she could only rely on the assistance of Peter de Brézé and his two thousand men. Setting sail early in October, she passed up the eastern coast, and landed in Northumberland, expecting that all the North Country would rise to her aid. No general insurrection followed, but Margaret's arrival was not without effect. Both Alnwick and Bamborough fell into her hands—the former by famine, for it was wholly unvictualled and could not hold out a week; the latter betrayed by the governor's brother. Nor was this all; the presence of the Queen moved the Scotch regents to break off their negotiations with England, and denounce the truce which they had so recently concluded. All that the statesmanship of Warwick and the sword of Montagu had done for England in the year 1462 was lost in the space of a week.

The moment that the unwelcome news of Margaret's advent reached London, Warwick flew to repair the disaster. Only eight days after the fall of Bamborough he was already at the head of twenty thousand men, and hastening north by forced marches. The King, ill-informed as to the exact force that had landed in Northumberland, had sent out in haste for every man that could be gathered, and followed himself with the full levy of the Southern Counties.

The nearer the Yorkists approached to the scene of action the less formidable did their task appear. The approach of winter had prevented the Scots from putting an army into the field, and the Lancastrians and their French allies had made no attempt to push out from their castles. All that they had done was to strengthen the three strongholds and fill them with provisions. In Alnwick lay Peter de Brézé's son and some of the Frenchmen, together with Lord Hungerford. Somerset, who had dropped his secret negotiations with Warwick when his mistress returned from France, held Bamborough; with him were Lord Roos and Jasper Earl of Pembroke. Sir Ralph Percy, the fighting-man of the Percy clan—for his nephew the heir of Northumberland was a minor—had made himself strong in Dunstanburgh. Meanwhile the Queen, on the approach of Warwick, had quitted her adherents and set sail for Scotland with her son and her treasure, under convoy of de Brézé and the main body of the French mercenaries. But the month was now November, the seas were rough, and off Bamborough she was caught in a storm; her vessel, with three others, was driven against the iron-bound coast, and she herself barely escaped with her life in a fishing-boat which took her into Berwick. Her treasures went to the bottom; and of her French followers four hundred were cast ashore on Holy Island, where they were forced to surrender next day to a force sent against them by Montagu.

Warwick had now arrived at Newcastle, and King Edward was but a few days' march behind him. Though the month was November, and winter campaigns, especially in the bleak and thinly-populated North, were in the fifteenth century as unusual as they were miserable, Warwick had determined to make an end of the new Lancastrian invasion before the Scots should have time to move. Luckily we have a full account of his dispositions for the simultaneous siege of the three Percy castles, from the pen of one who served on the spot.

The army was arranged as follows. King Edward with the reserve lay at Durham, in full touch with York and the South. The Duke of Norfolk held Newcastle, having as his main charge the duty of forwarding convoys of victuals and ammunition to the front, and of furnishing them with strong escorts on their way, to guard against any attempts made by roving bands of Scots or Percy retainers to break the line of communications, thirty miles long, which connected Newcastle with the army in the field. The force under Warwick's immediate command, charged with the reduction of the fortresses, was divided into four fractions. The castles lie at considerable intervals from each other: first, Bamborough to the north on a bold headland projecting into the sea, a Norman keep surrounded with later outworks; next Dunstanburgh, nine miles farther south, and also on the coast; lastly, Alnwick, five miles south-west of Dunstanburgh, on a hill, three miles from the seacoast, overlooking the river Alne. Dunstanburgh and Bamborough, if not relieved from the sea, could be surrounded and blockaded with comparative ease; Alnwick, the largest and strongest of the three castles, required to be shut in on all sides, and was likely to prove by far the hardest task. Luckily for Warwick the Roman road known as the Devil's Causeway was available for the connection of his outlying forces, as it runs almost by the walls of Alnwick and within easy distance of both Dunstanburgh and Bamborough. To each castle its own blockading force was attached. Opposite Bamborough, the one of the three which was nearest to Scotland and most exposed to attack by a relieving army, lay Montagu and Sir Robert Ogle, both of whom knew every inch of the Border. Dunstanburgh was beleaguered by Tiptoft Earl of Worcester and

Sir Ralph Grey. Alnwick was observed by Fauconbridge and Lord Scales. Warwick himself, with the general reserve, lay at Warkworth, three miles from Alnwick, ready to transfer himself to any point where his aid might be needed.

The forces employed were not less than thirty thousand men, without counting the troops on the lines of communication at Newcastle and Durham. To feed such a body in the depth of winter, in a sparsely-peopled and hostile country and with only one road open, was no mean task. Nevertheless the arrangements of Warwick worked with perfect smoothness and accuracy,—good witness to the fact that his talent for organisation was as great as his talent for the use of troops in the field. Every morning, we are told, the Earl rode out and visited all the three sieges "for to oversee; and if they wanted victuals or any other thing he was ready to purvey it to them with all his power." His day's ride was not less than thirty miles in all. The army was in good spirits and sure of success. "We have people enow here," wrote John Paston, whose duty it was to escort Norfolk's convoys to and fro, "so make as merry as ye can at home, for there is no jeopardie toward."

A siege at Christmastide was the last thing that the Lancastrians had expected at the moment of their rising; they had counted on having the whole winter to strengthen their position. No hope of immediate aid from Scotland was forthcoming, and after three weeks' blockade the spirits of the defenders of Bamborough and Dunstanburgh sank so low that they commenced to think of surrender. Somerset, as we have already mentioned, had been in treaty with Warwick six months before, with the object of obtaining grace from King Edward. He now renewed his offer to

Warwick, pledging himself to surrender Bamborough in return for a free pardon. Ralph Percy, the commander of Dunstanburgh, professed himself ready to make similar terms.

It is somewhat surprising to find that Warwick supported, and Edward granted, the petitions of Somerset and Percy. But it was now two years since the tragedy of Wakefield, both the King and his cousin were sincerely anxious to bring about a pacification, and they had resolved to forget their blood feud with the Beauforts. On Christmas Eve 1462, therefore, Bamborough and Dunstanburgh threw open their gates, such of their garrisons as chose to swear allegiance to King Edward being admitted to pardon, while the rest, headed by Jasper of Pembroke and Lord Roos, were allowed to retire to Scotland unarmed and with white staves in their hands. Somerset and Percy went on to Durham, where they swore allegiance to the King. Edward took them into favour and "gave them his own livery and great rewards," to Somerset in especial a grant of twenty marks a week for his personal expenses, and the promise of a pension of a thousand marks a year. As a token of his loyalty Somerset offered to take the field under Warwick against the Scots, and he was accordingly sent up to assist at the siege of Alnwick. Percy was shown equal favour; as a mark of confidence the King made him Governor of Bamborough which Somerset had just surrendered.

After the yielding of his chief adversary, King Edward thought that there was no further need for his presence in the North. Accordingly he returned home with the bulk of the army, leaving Warwick with ten thousand men, commanded by Norfolk and the Earl of Worcester, to finish the siege of Alnwick. Somerset lay with them, neither overmuch trusted nor overmuch contemned by his late enemies. Warwick's last siege, however, was not destined to come to such an uneventful close as those of Bamborough and Dunstanburgh. Lord Hungerford and the younger de Brézé made no signs of surrender, and protracted their defence till January 6th 1463.

On that day, at five o'clock in the dusk of the winter morning, a relieving army suddenly appeared in front of Warwick's entrenchments. Though it was mid-winter, Queen Margaret had succeeded in stirring up the Earl of Angus—the most powerful noble in Scotland and at that moment practical head of the Douglases—to lead a raid into England. Fired by the promise of an English dukedom, to be given when King Henry should come to his own again, Angus got together twenty thousand men, and slipping through the Central Marches, and taking to the Watling Street, presented himself most unexpectedly before the English camp. With him was Peter de Brézé, anxious to save his beleaguered son, and the Queen's French mercenaries.

For once in his life Warwick was taken by surprise. The Scots showed in such force that he thought himself unable to maintain the whole of his lines, and concentrated his forces on a front facing north-west between the castle hill and the river. Here he awaited attack, but nothing followed save insignificant skirmishing; Angus had come not to fight, but only to save the garrison. When the English blockading force was withdrawn, a party of Scotch horse rode up to the postern-gate of the castle and invited the besieged to escape; accordingly Lord Hungerford, the younger de Brézé, Sir Richard Tunstal, and the great majority of the garrison, hastily issued forth and joined the relieving force. Then Angus, to the surprise of the English, drew off his men, and fell back hastily over the Border.

Warwick had been quite out-generalled; but the whole of his fault seems to have been the neglect to keep a sufficient force of scouts on the Border. If he had known of Angus's approach, he would have been able to take proper measures for protecting the siege. But the main feeling in the English army was rather relief at the departure of the Scots than disgust at the escape of the garrison. "If on that day the Scots had but been bold as they were cunning, they might have destroyed the English lords, for they had double their numbers," writes the chronicler. The thing which attracted most notice was the fact that the renegade Somerset showed no signs of treachery, and bore himself bravely in the skirmish, "proving manfully that he was a true liegeman to King Edward." Henceforth he was trusted by his colleagues.

Some of the Alnwick garrison had been either unwilling or unable to escape with Angus. These protracted the defence for three weeks longer, but on January 30th they offered to surrender, and were allowed to depart unharmed to Scotland. The castle was garrisoned for the King, and entrusted to Sir John Ashley, to the great displeasure of Sir Ralph Grey to whom it had been promised. We shall see ere long what evils came from this displeasure.

It seemed now as if the war could not be far from its end. No single place now held out for Lancaster save the castle of Harlech in North Wales, where an obscure rebellion had been smouldering ever since 1461. We must not therefore blame Warwick for want of energy, when we find that in March he left the indefatigable

Montagu in command, and came up to London to attend the Parliament which King Edward had summoned to meet in April. Nevertheless, as we shall see, his absence had the most unhappy results on the Border.

We have no definite information as to Warwick's doings in the spring of 1463, but we cannot doubt that it was by his counsel and consent that in April his brother the Chancellor and his friend Lord Wenlock, in company with Bourchier Earl of Essex, went over-sea to Flanders, and contracted with Philip Duke of Burgundy a treaty of commercial intercourse and a political alliance. Philip then conveyed the English ambassadors to the Court of Louis of France, who was lying at Hesdin, and with him they negotiated a truce to last from October 1st till the new year. This was to be preliminary to a definite peace with France, a plan always forward in Warwick's thoughts, for he was convinced that the last hope of Lancaster lay in the support of Louis, and that peace between Edward and the French King would finally ruin Queen Margaret's plans.

But while George Neville and the Burgundians were negotiating, a new and curious development of this period of lingering troubles had commenced. Once more the Lancastrians were up in arms, and again the evil began in Northumberland. Sir Ralph Grey had been promised, as we mentioned above, the governorship of Alnwick, and had failed to receive it when the castle fell. This so rankled in his mind that he determined to risk his fortunes on an attempt to seize the place by force and deliver it up again to the Queen. In the end of May he mastered the castle by treachery, and sent for the Lancastrians from over the Border. Lord Hungerford came up, and once more received command of the castle which he had evacuated five months before. The news of this exploit of Grey's was too much for the loyalty of Sir Ralph Percy, the renegade governor of Bamborough. When de Brézé and Hungerford came before his gates he deliberately surrendered the castle to them without resistance.

The exasperating news that the North was once more aflame reached Warwick as he banqueted with King Edward at Westminster on May 31st. With his customary energy the Earl set himself to repair the mischief before it should spread farther. On June 2nd he was once more marching up the Great North Road, with a new commission to act as the King's lieutenant in the North, while his brother Montagu was named under him Lord Warden of the Marches. Warwick's plan of campaign this time was not to reduce the castles at once, but to cut off the Lancastrians from their base by forcing the Scots to conclude peace. Accordingly he left the strongholds on his right and made straight for the Border. His first exploit was to relieve Norham Castle, on the English side of the Tweed, which was beset by four thousand Scotch borderers, aided by Peter de Brézé and his mercenaries. Queen Margaret herself was in their camp, and had dragged her unfortunate consort down to the seat of war. When the English appeared, the Scots and French raised the siege and retired behind the Tweed, where they set themselves to guard the ford called the Holybank. But Warwick was determined to cross; he won the passage by force of arms, and drove off its defenders. A few miles across the Border he found de Brézé's Frenchmen resting in an abbey, and fell on them with such vehemence that several hundreds were taken prisoners, including the Lord of Graville and Raoul d'Araines, de Brézé's chief lieutenants.

One chronicler records a curious incident at this fight. "At the departing of Sir Piers de Bressy and his fellowship, there was one manly man among them, that purposed to meet with the Earl of Warwick; he was a taberette (drummer) and he stood upon a little hill with his tabor and his pipe, tabering and piping as merrily as any man might. There he stood by himself; till my lord Earl came unto him he would not leave his ground." Warwick was much pleased with the Frenchman's pluck, bade him be taken gently and well treated, "and there he became my lord's man, and yet is with him, a full good servant to his lord."

The moment that Warwick was actually across the Tweed, the Scotch regents offered him terms of peace. To prove their sincerity they agreed to send off Queen Margaret. Such pressure was accordingly put upon her that "she with all her Council, and Sir Peter with the Frenchmen, fled away by water in four balyngarys, and they landed at Sluis in Flanders, leaving all their horses and harness behind them, so sorely were they hasted by the Earl and his brother the Lord Montagu."[7] With the horses and harness was left poor King Henry, who for the next two years wandered about in an aimless way on both sides of the Border, a mere meaningless shadow now that he was separated from his vehement consort.

Now at last the Civil War seemed at an end. With Margaret oversea, Somerset a liegeman of York, the Northumbrian castles cut off from any hope of succour, and the Scots suing humbly for peace, Warwick might hope that his three years' toil had at last come to an end. That, after all, the struggle was to be protracted for twelve months more, was a fact that not even the best of prophets could have predicted.

After the raid which drove Queen Margaret away, and turned the hearts of the Scots toward peace, we lose sight of Warwick for some months. We only know that, for reasons to us unknown, he did not finish his exploits by the capture of the Northumbrian castles, but came home in the autumn, leaving them still unsubdued. Perhaps after the winter campaign of 1462-63 he wished to spend Christmas for once in his own fair castle of Warwick. His estates indeed in Wales and the West Midlands can hardly have seen him since the Civil War recommenced in 1459, and must have required the master's eye in every quarter. His wife and his daughters too, now girls growing towards a marriageable age as ages were reckoned in the fifteenth century, must long have been without a sight of him.

While Warwick was for once at home, and King Edward was making a progress round his kingdom with much pomp and expense, it would seem that Queen Margaret, from the retreat in Lorraine to which she had betaken herself, was once more exerting her influence to trouble England. At any rate a new Lancastrian conspiracy was hatched in the winter of 1463-64, with branches extending from Wales to Yorkshire. The outbreak commenced at Christmas by the wholly unexpected rebellion of the Duke of Somerset. Henry of Beaufort had been so well treated by King Edward that his conduct appears most extraordinary. He had supped at the King's board, slept in the King's chamber, served as captain of the King's guard, and jousted with the King's favour on his helm; yet at mid-winter he broke away for the North, with a very small following, and made for the garrison at Alnwick. Probably Somerset's conscience and his enemies had united to make his position unbearable. The Yorkists were always taunting him behind his back, and when he appeared in public in the King's company a noisy mob rose up to stone him, and Edward had much ado to save his life. But whether urged by remorse for his desertion of Lancaster, or by resentment for his treatment by the Yorkists, Somerset set himself to join the sinking cause at one of its darkest hours.

His arrival in the North, where he came almost alone, for his followers were wellnigh all cut off at Durham, was the signal for the new Lancastrian outbreak. Simultaneously Jasper of Pembroke endeavoured to stir up Wales. A rising took place in South Lancashire and Cheshire, in which at one moment ten thousand men are said to have been in the field: a band set out from Alnwick, pushed by the Yorkist garrison at Newcastle, and seized the Castle of Skipton in Craven, hard by Warwick's ancestral estates in the North Riding; and Norham on the Border was taken by treachery.

In March Warwick set out once more to regain the twice-subdued North. The rising in Cheshire collapsed without needing his arms to put it down, and he was able to reach York without molestation. From thence he sent to Scotland to summon the regency to carry out the terms of pacification which they had promised in the previous year. The Scots made no objection, and offered to send their ambassadors to York if safe escort was given them past the Lancastrian fortresses. Accordingly Montagu started from Durham to pick up his troops at Newcastle, where Lord

Scrope was already arrayed with the levies of the Northern Counties. This journey was near being Montagu's last, for a few miles outside Newcastle he was beset by his cousin Sir Humphrey Neville, the Earl of Westmoreland's nephew, who fell on his escort with eighty spears as he passed through a wood. Montagu, however, escaped by a detour and came safely into Newcastle, where he took charge of Scrope's force and marched for the Scotch Border.

At Hedgeley Moor he found Somerset with all the Lancastrian refugees barring the way. There had mustered all the survivors of the campaigns of 1461-2-3, Roos and Hungerford, and Tailboys Lord of Kyme, and the two traitors Ralph Grey and Ralph Percy. On April 15th their five thousand men fell on Montagu, whose forces were probably about equal. The shock was sharp but short; and when Ralph Percy, who led their van, was struck down, the Lancastrians dispersed. Percy, if the tale be true, refused to fly with the rest, and died crying, "I have saved the bird in my bosom," meaning his loyalty to Henry. He should have remembered his faith a year before, when he swore fealty to Edward at Durham.

Montagu was now able to reach Scotland unmolested. He brought the Scots Commissioners back to York, and a fifteen years' peace was safely concluded, the Scots promising to give no further shelter to the Lancastrians, and the English to disavow the Earls of Ross and Douglas whom they had armed against the Scotch regency. "An the Scots be true, the treaty may continue fifteen years," said the chronicler, "but it is hard to trust Scots: they be ever full of guile and deceit."

Somerset and his followers were now without hope. Their refuge in Scotland was cut off and their Northumbrian strongholds doomed to a speedy fall, for King Edward had been casting all the winter a train of great ordnance such as England had never seen before, and the pieces were already on their way north. Nevertheless the desperate adherents of Lancaster hardened their hearts, gathered their broken bands, and made one last desperate stand for the mastery of the North. On the Linhills, by the town of Hexham, they arrayed themselves against Montagu on May 13th. But when the Yorkists came in sight the hearts of the followers of Somerset failed them. All save five hundred melted away from their banners, and the small band that stayed to fight was broken, beaten, surrounded, and captured by Montagu's four thousand men with perfect ease.

The Lancastrian lords had fought their last field; one and all were slain or captured on the hill a mile outside Hexham town, where they had made their stand. Montagu marked his triumph by the most bloody executions that had been seen throughout the whole war. At Hexham, next day, he beheaded Somerset, Sir Edmond Fitzhugh, a moss-trooping captain called Black Jack, and three more. On the next day but one he slew at Newcastle Lord Roos, Lord Hungerford, and three others. Next day he moved south to his brother's ancestral seat of Middleham, and executed Sir Philip Wentworth and six squires. Finally, he conducted to York and beheaded there Sir Thomas Hussey and thirteen more, the remainder of the prisoners of rank who had come into his hands.

For these sweeping executions Warwick must take part of the blame. But there is this to be said in defence of Montagu's stern justice, that Somerset and three or four others of the victims were men who had claimed and abused Edward's pardon, and that Roos and several more had been spared at the surrender of Bamborough in 1462. The whole body had shown that they could never be trusted, even if they professed to submit to York; and the practical justification of their death lies in the fact that with their execution ceased all attempts to raise the North in favour of the house of Lancaster. Public opinion among the Yorkists had nothing but praise for Montagu. "Lo, so manly a man is this good Lord Montagu," wrote a London chronicler, "he spared not their malice, nor their falseness, nor their guile, nor their treason, but slew many, and took many, and let smite off their heads"!

Even before the battle of Hedgeley Moor King Edward had set out to reinforce Warwick and Montagu. The news of their victories reached him on the way, but he continued to advance, bringing with him the great train of artillery destined for the siege of the Northumbrian fortresses. This journey was important to King Edward in more ways than one. How he spent one day of it, May 1st, when he lay at Stony Stratford, we shall presently see. If Warwick had but known of his master's doings on that morning, we may doubt if he would have been so joyous over his brother's victories or so remorseless with his captured enemies.

The King came up to York in the end of May, "and kept his estate there solemnly in the palace, and there he created John Lord Montagu Earl of Northumberland," in memory of his good service during the last few months, handing over to him, together with the

Percy title, the greater part of the great Percy estates—Alnwick and Warkworth and Langley and Prudhoe, and many more fiefs between Tyne and Tweed.

Warwick now advanced northward to complete the work which his brother had begun in the previous month, while the King remained behind in Yorkshire and occupied himself in the capture of Skipton Castle in Craven. On June 23rd the Earl appeared before Alnwick and summoned the place. The Lancastrians had lost their leaders at Hexham, there was no more fight in them, and they surrendered at once on promise of their lives. Dunstanburgh and Norham followed the example of Alnwick. Only Bamborough held out, for there Sir Ralph Grey had taken refuge. He knew that his treachery at Alnwick in the last year could never be pardoned, and utterly refused to surrender. With him was Sir Humphrey Neville, who had so nearly destroyed Montagu two months before.

We happen to have an account of the siege of Bamborough which is not without its interest. When the army appeared before the castle Warwick's herald summoned it in form—

Offering free pardon, grace, body, and livelihood to all, reserving two persons, Sir Ralph Grey and Sir Humphrey Neville. Then Sir Ralph clearly determined within himself to live or die within the place, though the herald charged him with all inconvenience and shedding of blood that might befall: saying in this wise: "My Lord ensureth you upon his honour to sustain this siege before you these seven years so that he win you: and if ye deliver not this jewel, which the King our dread Sovereign Lord hath greatly in favour, seeing it marches so nigh unto his enemies of Scotland, whole and unbroken with ordnance, and if ye suffer any great guns to be laid against it, it shall cost you a head for every gun shot, from the head of the chief man to the head of the least person within." But Sir Ralph departed from the herald, and put him in endeavour to make defence.

Warwick was therefore compelled to have recourse to his battering train, the first that had been used to effect in an English siege.

So all the King's guns that were charged began to shoot upon the said castle. "Newcastle," the King's greatest gun, and "London," the second gun of iron, so betide the place that the stones of the walls flew into the sea. "Dijon," a brass gun of the King's, smote through Sir Ralph Grey's chamber oftentimes, and "Edward" and "Richard," the bombardels, and other ordnance, were busied on the place. Presently the wall was breached, and my lord of Warwick, with his men-at-arms and archers, won the castle by assault, maugre Sir Ralph Grey, and took him alive, and brought him to the King at Doncaster. And there the Earl of Worcester, Constable of England, sat in judgment on him.

Tiptoft was a judge who never spared, and Grey a renegade who could expect no mercy. The prisoner was sentenced to be beheaded, and only spared degradation from his knighthood "because of his noble ancestor, who suffered at Southampton for the sake of the King's grandfather, Richard Earl of Cambridge." His head was sent to join the ghastly collection standing over the gate on London Bridge.

With the fall of Bamborough the first act of King Edward's reign was at an end.

Footnotes

6. Queen Mary had, so the story runs, shown overmuch favour to the Duke of Somerset. He openly boasted of his success in love, and the Queen was ever after his deadly enemy.

7. The famous story of the robber and Queen Margaret, placed by so many writers after the battle of Hexham, seems quite impossible. If the incident took place at all, it happened on the other side of the Channel.

Chapter 13

THE QUARREL OF WARWICK AND KING EDWARD

With Hedgeley Moor and Hexham and the final surrender of the Northumbrian castles ended the last desperate attempt of the Lancastrians to hold their own in the North. The few surviving leaders who had escaped the fate of Somerset and Hungerford left Scotland and fled over-sea. Philip de Commines soon after met the chief of them in the streets of Ghent "reduced to such extremity of want and poverty that no common beggar could have been poorer. The Duke of Exeter was seen (though he concealed his name) following the Duke of Burgundy's train begging his bread from door to door, till at last he had a small pension allowed him in pity for his subsistence." With him were some of the Somersets, John and Edmund, brothers of the Duke who had just been beheaded. Jasper of Pembroke made his way to Wales and wandered in the hills from county to county, finding friends nowhere. No one could have guessed that the cause of Lancaster would ever raise its head again.

The times of war were at length over, and Warwick, like the rest of Englishmen, might begin to busy himself about other things than battles and sieges. In July he was at last free, and was able to think of turning southward to seek for more than a passing visit the Midland estates of which he had seen so little for the last five years. After a short interval of leisure, we find him in September sitting in the King's Council, and urging on two measures which he held necessary for the final pacification of the realm. The first was the conclusion of a definite treaty of peace with France. It was from King Louis that the Lancastrians had been accustomed to draw their supplies of ships and money, and while England and France were still at war it was certain that King Edward's enemies would continue to obtain shelter and succour across the Channel. Accordingly the Earl urged on the conclusion of a treaty, and finally procured the appointment of himself and his friend and follower Wenlock as ambassadors to Louis. The second point of his schemes was connected with the first. It was high time, as all England had for some time been saying, that the King should marry.[8] Edward was now in his twenty-fourth year, "and men marvelled that he abode so long without any wife, and feared that he was not over chaste of his living." Those, indeed, who were about the King's person knew that some scandal had already been caused by his attempts, successful and unsuccessful, on the honour of several ladies about the Court. Rumour had for some time been coupling Edward's name with that of various princesses of a marriageable age among foreign royal families. Some had said that he was about to marry Mary of Gueldres, the Queen Dowager of Scotland, and others had speculated on his opening negotiations for the hand of Isabel of Castile, sister of the reigning Spanish King. But there had been no truth in these reports. Warwick's scheme was to cement the peace with France by a marriage with a French princess, and in the preliminary inquiries which the King permitted him to send to Louis the marriage question was distinctly mentioned. Louis' sisters were all married, and his daughters were mere children, so that their names were not brought forward, for King Edward required a wife of suitable years, "to raise him goodly lineage such as his father had reared." The lady whom Warwick proposed to the King was Bona of Savoy, sister to Charlotte Queen of France, a princess who dwelt at her brother-in-law King Louis' Court and in whose veins ran the blood both of the Kings of France and the Dukes of Burgundy.

King Edward made no open opposition to Warwick's plans. The project was mooted to King Louis, safe conducts for the English Embassy were obtained, and Warwick and Wenlock were expected at St. Omer about October 3rd or 4th. But at the last moment, when Warwick attended at Reading on September 28th to receive his master's final instructions, a most astounding announcement was made to him. We have an account of the scene which bears some marks of truth.

The Council met for the formal purpose of approving the marriage negotiations. A speaker, probably Warwick, laid before the King the hope and expectation of his subjects that he would deign to give them a Queen.

Then the King answered that of a truth he wished to marry, but that perchance his choice might not be to the liking of all present. Then those of his Council asked to know of his intent, and would be told to what house he would go. To which the King replied in right merry guise that he would take to wife Dame Elizabeth Grey, the daughter of Lord Rivers. But they answered him that she was not his match, however good and however fair she might be, and that he must know well that she was no wife for such a high prince as himself; for she was not the daughter of a duke or earl, but her mother the Duchess of Bedford had married a simple knight, so that though she was the child of a duchess and the niece of the Count of St. Pol, still she was no wife for him. When King Edward heard these sayings of the lords of his blood and his Council, which it seemed good to them to lay before him, he answered that he should have no other wife and that such was his good pleasure.

Then came the clinching blow; no other wife could he have—for he was married to Dame Elizabeth already!

In fact, five months before, on May 1st, when he ought to have been far on his way to the North, King Edward had secretly ridden over from Stony Stratford to Grafton in Northamptonshire, and wedded the lady. No one had suspected the marriage, for the King had had but a short and slight acquaintance with Elizabeth Grey, who had been living a retired life ever since her husband, a Lancastrian knight, fell in the moment of victory at the second battle of St. Albans. Edward had casually met her, had been conquered by her fair face, and had made hot love to her. Elizabeth was clever and cautious; she would hear of nothing but a formal offer of marriage, and the young King, perfectly infatuated by his passion, had wedded her in secret at Grafton in the presence of no one save her mother and two other witnesses. This was the urgent private business which had kept him from appearing to open his Parliament at York.

The marriage was a most surprising event. Lord Rivers, the lady's father, had been a keen Lancastrian. He it was who had been captured at Sandwich in 1460, and brought before Warwick and Edward to undergo that curious scolding which we have elsewhere recorded. And now this "made lord, who had won his fortune by his marriage," had become the King's father-in-law. Dame

Elizabeth herself was seven years older than her new husband, and was the mother of children twelve and thirteen years of age. The public was so astonished at the match that it was often said that the Queen's mother, the old Duchess of Bedford, must have given King Edward a love philtre, for in no other way could the thing be explained.

Warwick and the rest of the lords of the Council were no less vexed than astonished by this sudden announcement. The Earl had broached the subject of the French marriage to King Louis, and was expected to appear within a few days to submit the proposal for acceptance. The King, knowing all the time that the scheme was impossible, had allowed him to commit himself to it, and now left him to explain to King Louis that he had been duped in the most egregious way, and had been excluded from his master's confidence all along. Very naturally the Earl let the embassy drop; he could not dare to appear before the French King to ask for peace, when the bond of union which he had promised to cement it was no longer possible.

But vexed and angered though he must have been at the way in which he had been treated, Warwick was too loyal a servant of the house of York to withdraw from his master's Council. He bowed to necessity, and acquiesced in what he could not approve. Accordingly Warwick attended next day to hear the King make public announcement of his marriage in Reading Abbey on the feast of St. Michael, and he himself, in company with George of Clarence the King's brother, led Dame Elizabeth up to the seat prepared for her beside her husband, and bowed the knee to her as Queen.

For a few months it seemed as if the King's marriage had been a single freak of youthful passion, and the domination of the house of Neville in the royal Councils appeared unshaken. As if to make amends for his late treatment of Warwick, Edward raised his brother George Neville the Chancellor to the vacant Archbishopric of York, and in token of confidence sent the Earl as his representative to prorogue a Parliament summoned to meet on November 4th.

But these marks of regard were not destined to continue. The favours of the King, though there was as yet no open breach between him and his great Minister, were for the future bestowed in another quarter. The house of Rivers was almost as prolific as the house of Neville; the Queen had three brothers, five sisters, and two sons, and for them the royal influence was utilised in the most extraordinary way during the next two years. Nor was it merely inordinate affection for his wife that led King Edward to squander his wealth and misuse his power for the benefit of her relatives. It soon became evident that he had resolved to build up with the aid of the Queen's family one of those great allied groups of noble houses whose strength the fifteenth century knew so well—a group that should make him independent of the control of the Nevilles. A few days after the acknowledgment of the Queen, began a series of marriages in the Rivers family, which did not cease for two years. In October 1464, immediately after the scene at Reading, the Queen's sister Margaret was married to Thomas Lord Maltravers, the heir of the wealthy Earl of Arundel. In January 1465 John Woodville, the youngest of her brothers, wedded the Dowager Duchess of Norfolk. This was a disgraceful match: the bridegroom was just of age, the bride quite old enough to be his grandmother; but she was a great heiress, and the King persuaded her to marry the sordid young man. Within eighteen months more, nearly the whole of the family had been married off: Anne Woodville to the heir of Bourchier Earl of Essex; Mary Woodville to the eldest son of Lord Herbert, the King's most intimate counsellor after Warwick in his earlier years; Eleanor Woodville to George Grey heir of the Earl of Kent; and Catherine Woodville, most fortunate of all, to the young Duke of Buckingham, grandson of the old Duke who had fallen at Northampton. To end the tale of the alliances of this most fortunate family, it is only necessary to add that even before Queen Elizabeth's marriage her eldest brother Anthony had secured the hand of Elizabeth, heiress of the Lord Scales who was slain on the Thames in 1460. Truly the Woodville marriages may compare not unfavourably with those of the Nevilles!

While the King was heaping his favours on the house of Rivers, Warwick was still employed from time to time in the service of the Crown. But he could no longer feel that he had the chief part in guiding his monarch's policy. Indeed, the King seems to have even gone out of his way to carry out every scheme on a different principle from that which the Earl adopted. In the spring of 1465, at the time of the Queen's formal coronation in May—a ceremony which he was glad enough to escape—Warwick went over-sea to conduct negotiations with the French and Burgundians. He met the Burgundian ambassadors at Boulogne, and those of France at Calais. It was a critical time for both France and Burgundy, for the War of the Public Weal had just broken out, and each party was anxious to secure the friendship, or at least the neutrality of England. With the Burgundians, whom Warwick met first, no agreement could be made, for the Count of Charolois, who had now got the upper hand of his aged father Duke Philip, refused to make any pledges against helping the Lancastrians. He was at this very time pensioning the exiled Somersets and Exeter, and almost reckoned himself a Lancastrian prince, because his mother, Isabel of Portugal, was a grand-daughter of John of Gaunt. Warwick and Charles of Charolois were quite unable to agree. Each of them was too much accustomed to have his own way, and though they held high feasts together at Boulogne, and were long in council, they parted in wrath. There would seem to have been something more than a mere difference of opinion between them, for ever afterwards they regarded each other as personal enemies. King Louis, whose ambassadors met Warwick a month later, proved far more accommodating than the hot-headed Burgundian prince. He consented to forget the matter of the marriage, and agreed to the conclusion of a truce for eighteen months, during which he engaged to give no help to Queen Margaret, while Warwick covenanted that England should refrain from aiding the Dukes of Burgundy and Bretagne, now in full rebellion against their sovereign.

Late in the summer of 1465 Warwick returned home just in time to hear of a new stroke of fortune which had befallen his master. Henry the Sixth had just been captured in Lancashire. The ex-king had wandered down from his retreat in Scotland, and was moving about in an aimless way from one Lancastrian household to another, accompanied by no one but a couple of priests. One of

Henry's entertainers betrayed him, and he was seized by John Talbot of Basshall as he sat at meat in Waddington Hall, and forwarded under guard to London. At Islington Warwick rode forth to meet his late sovereign, and by the King's orders led him publicly through the city, with his feet bound by leather straps to his stirrups. Why this indignity was inflicted on the unfortunate Henry it is hard to say; there cannot possibly have been any fear of a rescue, and Warwick might well have spared his late master the shame of bonds. Henry was led along Cheapside and Cornhill to the Tower, where he was placed in honourable custody, and permitted to receive the visits of all who wished to see him.

That Warwick was not yet altogether out of favour with King Edward was shown by the fact that he was asked to be godfather to the Queen's first child, the Princess Elizabeth, in the February of the following year 1466. But immediately afterwards came the succession of events which marked the final breach between the King and the Nevilles. In March Edward suddenly dismissed from the office of Treasurer Lord Mountjoy, a friend of Warwick's, and gave the post to his wife's father Lord Rivers, whom he soon created an earl. The removal of his friend was highly displeasing to Warwick; but worse was to follow. Warwick's nephew George Neville, the heir of his brother John, had been affianced to Anne heiress of the exiled Duke of Exeter; but the Queen gave the Duchess of Exeter four thousand marks to break off the match, and the young lady was wedded to Thomas Grey, Elizabeth's eldest son by her first marriage. This blow struck the Nevilles in their tenderest point; even the marriages which had made their good fortune were for the future to be frustrated by royal influence.

The next slight which Warwick received at the hands of his sovereign touched him even more closely. His eldest daughter Isabel, who had been born in 1451, was now in her sixteenth year, and already thoughts about her marriage had begun to trouble her father's brain. The Earl counted her worthy of the highest match that could be found in the realm, for there was destined to go with her hand such an accumulation of estates as no subject had ever before possessed—half of the lands of Neville, Montacute, Despenser, and Beauchamp. The husband whom Warwick had hoped to secure for his child was George Duke of Clarence, the King's next brother, a young man of eighteen years. Clarence was sounded, and liked the prospect well enough, for the young lady was fair as well as rich. But they had not reckoned with the King. After a long visit which Clarence and his younger brother Richard of Gloucester had paid to Warwick in the end of 1466, Edward got wind of the proposed marriage. "When the King knew that his brothers had returned from their visit to the Earl at Cambridge, he asked them why they had left his Court, and who had given them counsel to visit the Earl. Then they answered that none had been the cause save they themselves. And the King asked whether there had been any talk of affiancing them to their cousins, the Earl's daughters; and the Duke of Clarence"—always prompt at a lie—"answered that there was not. But the King, who had been fully informed of all, waxed wroth, and sent them from his presence." Edward strictly forbade the marriage, and for the present there was no more talk of it; but Clarence and Warwick understood each other, and were always in communication, much to the King's displeasure. It did not please him to find his heir presumptive and his most powerful subject on too good terms.

The King waited a few months more, and then proceeded to put a far worse insult on his old friends and followers. In May 1467 he sent Warwick over-sea, with a commission to visit the King of France, and turn the eighteen months truce made in 1465 into a permanent peace on the best terms possible. The errand seemed both useful and honourable, and Warwick went forth in good spirits; but it was devised in reality merely to get him out of the kingdom, at a time when the King was about to cross all his most cherished plans.

Louis was quite as desirous as Warwick himself to conclude a permanent peace. It was all-important to him that England should not be on the side of Burgundy, and he was ready to make the Earl's task easy. The reception which he prepared for Warwick was such as might have been given to a crowned head. He went five leagues down the Seine to receive the English embassy, and feasted Warwick royally on the river bank. When Rouen was reached "the King gave the Earl most honourable greeting; for there came out to meet him the priests of every parish in the town in their copes, with crosses and banners and holy water, and so he was conducted to Notre Dame de Rouen, where he made his offering. And he was well lodged at the Jacobins in the said town of Rouen. Afterward the Queen and her daughters came to the said town that he might see them. And the King abode with Warwick for the space of twelve days communing with him, after which the Earl departed back into England." And with him went as Ambassadors from France the Archbishop of Narbonne, the

Bastard of Bourbon (Admiral of France), the Bishop of Bayeux, Master Jean de Poupencourt, and William Monipenny, a Scotch agent in whom the King placed much confidence.

Warwick and the French Ambassadors landed at Sandwich, where they had a hearty reception; for the people of Sandwich, like all the men of Kent, were great supporters of the Earl. Posts were sent forward to notify their arrival to the King, and the party then set out to ride up to London. As they drew near the city the Earl was somewhat vexed to find that no one came forth to welcome them on the King's behalf; but presently the Duke of Clarence came riding alone to meet him, and brought him intelligence which turned his satisfaction at the success of the French negotiations into bitter vexation of spirit.

When Warwick had got well over-sea, the King had proceeded to work out his own plans, secure that he would not be interrupted. He had really determined to make alliance with Burgundy and not with France; and the moment that the coast was clear a Burgundian emissary appeared in London. Antony "the Grand Bastard," the trusted agent of the Court of Charolois, ascended the Thames at the very moment that Warwick was ascending the Seine. Ostensibly he came on a chivalrous errand, to joust with the Queen's brother Lord Scales in honour of all the ladies of Burgundy. The passage of arms was duly held, to the huge delight of the populace of London, and the English chroniclers give us all its details—instead of relating the important political events of the year. But the real object of the Bastard's visit was to negotiate an English alliance for his brother; and he was so successful that he returned to Flanders authorised to promise the hand of the King's sister Margaret to the Count of Charolois.

But Warwick had not merely to learn that the King had stultified his negotiations with France by making an agreement with Burgundy behind his back. He was now informed that, only two days before his arrival, Edward had gone, without notice given or cause assigned, to his brother the Archbishop of York, who lay ill at his house by Westminster Barrs, and suddenly dismissed him from the Chancellorship and taken the great seal from him. Open war had been declared on the house of Neville.[9]

But bitterly vexed though he was at his sovereign's double dealing, Warwick proceeded to carry out the forms of his duty. He called on the King immediately on his arrival, announced the success of his embassy, and craved for a day of audience for the French Ambassadors. "When the Earl spoke of all the good cheer that King Louis had made him, and how he had sent him the keys of every castle and town that he passed through, he perceived from the King's countenance that he was paying no attention at all to what he was saying, so he betook himself home, sore displeased."

Next day the French had the audience. The King received them in state, surrounded by Rivers, Scales, John Woodville, and Lord Hastings. "The Ambassadors were much abashed to see him, for he showed himself a prince of a haughty bearing." Warwick then introduced them, and Master Jean de Poupencourt, as spokesman for the rest, laid the proposals of Louis before the King. Edward briefly answered that he had pressing business, and could not communicate with them himself; they might say their say to certain lords whom he would appoint for the purpose. Then they were ushered out of his presence. It was clear that he would do nothing for them; indeed the whole business had only been concocted to get Warwick out of the way. It was abortive, and had been intended to be so.

The Earl on leaving the palace was bursting with rage; his ordinary caution and affability were gone, and he broke out in angry words even before the foreigners. "As they rowed home in their barge the Frenchmen had many discourses with each other. But Warwick was so wroth that he could not contain himself, and he said to the Admiral of France, 'Have you not seen what traitors there are about the King's person?' But the Admiral answered, 'My Lord, I pray you grow not hot; for some day you shall be well avenged.' But the Earl said, 'Know that those very traitors were the men who have had my brother displaced from the office of Chancellor, and made the King take the seal from him.'"

Edward went to Windsor next day, taking no further heed of the Ambassadors. He appointed no one to treat with them, and they remained six weeks without hearing from him, seeing no one but Warwick, who did his best to entertain them, and Warwick's new ally the Duke of Clarence. At last they betook themselves home, having accomplished absolutely nothing. On the eve of their departure the King sent them a beggarly present of hunting-horns, leather bottles, and mastiffs, in return for the golden hanaps and bowls and the rich jewellery which they had brought from France.

Warwick would have nothing more to do with his master. He saw the Ambassadors back as far as Sandwich, and then went off in high dudgeon to Middleham. There he held much deep discourse with his brothers, George the dispossessed Chancellor, and John of Montagu the Earl of Northumberland. At Christmas the King summoned him to Court; he sent back the reply that "never would he come again to Council while all his mortal enemies, who were about the King's person, namely, Lord Rivers the Treasurer, and Lord Scales and Lord Herbert and Sir John Woodville, remained there present." The breach between Warwick and his master was now complete.

Footnotes

8. There seems to be no foundation for the theory that Warwick wished the King to marry his daughter Isabel. The Earl moved strongly in favour of the French marriage, and his daughter was too young, being only thirteen years of age, for a king desirous of raising up heirs to his crown.

9. It seems impossible to work out to any purpose the statement of Polidore Vergil and others that Warwick's final breach with the King was caused by Edward's offering violence to a lady of the house of Neville. Lord Lytton, of course, was justified in using this hint for his romance, but the historian finds it too vague and untrustworthy.

Chapter 14

PLAYING WITH TREASON

Great ministers who have been accustomed to sway the destinies of kingdoms, and who suddenly find themselves disgraced at their master's caprice, have seldom been wont to sit down in resignation and accept their fall with equanimity. Such a line of conduct requires a self-denial and a high-flown loyalty to principle which are seldom found in the practical statesman. If the fallen minister is well stricken in years, and the fire has gone out of him, he may confine himself to sermons on the ingratitude of kings. If his greatness has been purely official, and his power entirely dependent on the authority entrusted to him by his master, his discontent may not be dangerous. But Warwick was now in the very prime of his life,—he was just forty,—and he was moreover by far the most powerful subject within the four seas. It was sheer madness in King Edward to goad such a man to desperation by a series of deliberate insults.

This was no mere case of ordinary ingratitude. If ever one man had made another, Richard Neville had made Edward Plantagenet. He had taken charge of him, a raw lad of eighteen, at the moment of the disastrous rout of Ludford, and trained him in arms and statecraft with unceasing care. Twice had he saved the lost cause of York, in 1459 and in 1461. He had spent five years in harness, in one long series of battles and sieges, that his cousin might wear his crown in peace. He had compassed sea and land in embassies that Edward might be safe from foreign as well as from domestic foes. He had seen his father and his brother fall by the axe and the sword in the cause of York. He had seen his mother and his wife fugitives on the face of the earth, his castles burnt, his manors wasted, his tenants slain, all that the son of Richard Plantagenet might sit on the throne that was his father's due.

Warwick then might well be cut to the heart at his master's ingratitude. It was no marvel if, after the King's last treachery to him in the matter of the French embassy, he retired from Court and sent a bitter answer to Edward's next summons. After the open breach there were now two courses open to him: the first to abandon all his schemes, and betake himself in silent bitterness to the management of his vast estates; the second was to endeavour to win his way back to power by the ways which medieval England knew only too well—the way which had served Simon de Montfort, and Thomas of Lancaster, and Richard of York; the way that had led Simon and Thomas and Richard to their bloody graves. The first alternative was no doubt the one that the perfect man, the ideally loyal and unselfish knight, should have chosen. But Richard Neville was no perfect man; he was a practical statesman—"the cleverest man of his time," says one who had observed him closely; and his long tenure of power had made him look upon the first place in the Council of the King as his right and due. His enemies the Woodvilles and Herberts had driven him from his well-earned precedence by the weapons that they could use—intrigue and misrepresentation; what more natural than that he should repay them by the weapon that he could best employ, the iron hand of armed force?

Hitherto the career of Warwick had been singularly straightforward and consistent. Through thick and thin he had supported the cause of York and never wavered in his allegiance to it. It must not be supposed that he changed his whole policy when his quarrel with the King came to a head. As his conduct in 1469, when his ungrateful master was in his power, was destined to show, he had no further design than to reconquer for himself the place in the royal Council which had been his from 1461 to 1464. Later events developed his plans further than he had himself expected, but it is evident that at first his sole design was to clear away the Woodvilles. The only element in his programme which threatened to lead to deeper and more treasonable plans was his connection with his would-be son-in-law George of Clarence. The handsome youth who professed such a devotion to him, followed his advice with such docility, and took his part so warmly in the quarrel with the King, seems from the first to have obtained a place in his affections greater than Edward had ever won. But Clarence had his ambitions; what they were and how far they extended the Earl had not as yet discovered.

Warwick had now the will to play his master's new ministers an ill turn; that he had also the power to do so none knew better than himself. The lands of Neville and Montacute, Beauchamp and Despenser united could send into the field a powerful army. Moreover, his neighbours, in most of the counties where his influence prevailed, had bound themselves to him by taking his livery; barons as well as knights were eager to be of his "Privy Council," to wear his Ragged Staff and ride in his array. The very aspect of his household seemed to show the state of a petty king.

Every one has read Hollingshead's famous description, which tells how the little army of followers which constituted his ordinary retinue eat six oxen daily for breakfast.

Nor was it only in the strength of his own retainers that Warwick trusted; he knew that he himself was the most popular man in the kingdom. Men called him ever the friend of the Commons, and "his open kitchen persuaded the meaner sort as much as the justice of his cause." His adversaries, on the other hand, were unmistakably disliked by the people. The old partisans of York still looked on the Woodvilles as Lancastrian renegades, and the grasping avarice of Rivers and his family was stirring up popular demonstration against them even before Warwick's breach with the King. A great mob in Kent had sacked one of Rivers' manors and killed his deer in the autumn of 1467, and trouble was brewing against him in other quarters. A word of summons from Warwick would call rioters out of the ground in half the shires of England. Already in January 1468 a French ambassador reports: "In one county more than three hundred archers were in arms, and had made themselves a captain named Robin, and sent to the Earl of Warwick to know if it was time to be busy, and to say that all their neighbours were ready. But my Lord answered, bidding them go home, for it was not yet time to be stirring. If the time should come, he would let them know."[10]

It was not only discontented Yorkists that had taken the news of the quarrel between Warwick and his master as a signal for moving. The tidings had stirred the exiled Lancastrians to a sudden burst of activity of which we should hardly have thought them capable. Queen Margaret borrowed ships and money from Louis, and lay in force at Harfleur. Sir Henry Courtney, heir of the late Earl of Devon, and Thomas Hungerford, son of the lord who fell at Hexham, tried to raise an insurrection in the South-West; but they were caught by Lord Stafford of Southwick and beheaded at Salisbury. As a reward the King gave Stafford his victim's title of Earl of Devon. In Wales the long-wandering Jasper Tudor suddenly appeared, at the head of two thousand men, supported by a small French fleet. He took Harlech Castle and sacked Denbigh; but a few weeks later Warwick's enemy, Lord Herbert, fell upon him at the head of the Yorkists of the March, routed his tumultuary army, retook Harlech, and forced him again to seek refuge in the hills. Herbert, like Lord Stafford, was rewarded with the title of the foe he had vanquished, and became Earl of Pembroke. While these risings were on foot, Lancastrian emissaries were busy all over England; but their activity only resulted in a series of executions. Two gentlemen of the Duke of Norfolk's retinue were beheaded for holding secret communication with the Beauforts while they were in Flanders, following the train which escorted the Princess Margaret at her marriage with Charles of Charolois, who had now become Duke of Burgundy. In London more executions took place, and Sir Thomas Cooke, late Lord Mayor, had all his goods confiscated for misprision of treason. Two of the Lancastrian emissaries alleged, under torture, the one, that Warwick had promised aid to the rising, the other that Lord Wenlock, Warwick's friend and supporter, had guilty knowledge of the scheme; but in each case the King himself acknowledged that the accusation was frivolous—the random imagining of men on the rack, forced to say something to save their own bones. It was not likely that Warwick would play the game of Queen Margaret, the slayer of his father and brother, and the instigator of attempts on his own life.

Startled by the sudden revival of Lancastrian energy, but encouraged by the easy way in which he had mastered it, King Edward determined to give the war-like impulses of his subjects vent by undertaking in the next year a great expedition against France. He had the example of Henry the Fifth before his eyes, and hoped to stifle treason at home by foreign war. Among his preparations for leaving home was a determined attempt to open negotiations with Warwick for a reconciliation. The King won over the Archbishop of York to plead his cause, by restoring to him some estates which he had seized in 1467; and about Easter George Neville induced his brother to meet the King at Coventry. Warwick came, but it is to be feared that he came fully resolved to have his revenge at his own time, with his heart quite unsoftened toward his master; yet he spoke the King fair, and even consented to be reconciled to Lord Herbert, though he would have nothing to say to the Woodvilles. He was also induced to join the company which escorted the Princess Margaret to the coast, on her way to her marriage in Flanders. After this Warwick paid a short visit to London, where he sat among the judges who in July tried the Lancastrian conspirators of the city. Clarence accompanied him, and sat on the same bench. He had spent the last few months in moving the Pope to grant him a disposition to marry Isabel Neville,[11] for they were within the prohibited degrees; but under pressure from King Edward the Curia had delayed the consideration of his request.

The autumn of 1468 and the spring of 1469 passed away quietly. Warwick made no movement, for he was still perfecting his plans. He saw with secret pleasure that the French, with whom peace would have been made long ago if his advice had been followed, kept the King fully employed. It must have given him peculiar gratification when his enemy Anthony Woodville, placed at the head of a large fleet, made two most inglorious expeditions to the French coast, and returned crestfallen without having even seen the enemy.

Meanwhile the Earl had been quietly measuring his resources. He had spoken to all his kinsmen, and secured the full co-operation of the majority of them. George the Archbishop of York, Henry Neville heir to Warwick's aged uncle Lord Latimer, Sir John Coniers of Hornby, husband of his niece Alice Neville, his cousin Lord Fitzhugh, and Thomas "the bastard of Fauconbridge," natural son to the deceased peer who had fought so well at Towton, were his chief reliance. His brother John of Montagu, the Earl of Northumberland, could not make up his mind; he did not reveal Warwick's plans to the King, but he would not promise any aid. William Neville of Abergavenny was now too old to be taken into account. The rest of Warwick's uncles and brothers were by this time dead.

By April 1469 the preparations were complete. Every district where the name of Neville was great had been carefully prepared for trouble. Kent, Yorkshire, and South Wales were ready for insurrection, and yet all had been done so quietly that the King, who ever since he had thrown off the Earl's influence had been sinking deeper and deeper into habits of careless evil-living and debauchery, suspected nothing.

In April Warwick took his wife and daughters across to Calais, apparently to get them out of harm's way. He himself, professing a great wish to see his cousin Margaret, the newly-married Duchess of Burgundy, went on to St. Omer. He there visited Duke Charles, and was reconciled to him in spite of the evil memories of their last meeting at Boulogne. To judge from his conduct, the Earl was bent on nothing but a harmless tour; but, as a matter of fact, his movements were but a blind destined to deceive King Edward. While he was feasting at St. Omer he had sent orders over-sea for the commencement of an insurrection. In a few days it was timed to break out. Meanwhile Warwick returned to Calais, and lodged with Wenlock, who was in charge of the great fortress.

His orders had had their effect. In the end of June grave riots broke out in the neighbourhood of York. Ostensibly they were connected with the maladministration of the estates of St. Leonard's hospital in that city; but they were in reality political and not agrarian. Within a few days fifteen thousand men were at the gates of York, clamorously setting forth a string of grievances, which were evidently founded on Cade's manifesto of 1450. Once more we hear of heavy taxation, maladministration of the law, the alienation of the royal estates to upstart favourites, the exclusion from the royal Councils of the great lords of the royal blood. Once more a demand is made for the punishment of evil counsellors, and the introduction of economy into the royal household, and the application of the revenue to the defence of the realm. The first leader of the rioters was Robert Huldyard, known as Robin of

Redesdale, no doubt the same Robin whom the Earl had bidden in 1468 to keep quiet and wait the appointed time. John Neville the Earl of Northumberland lay at York with a large body of men-at-arms, for he was still Lieutenant of the North. Many expected that he would join the rioters; but, either because he had not quite recognised the insurrection to be his brother's work, or because he had resolved to adhere loyally to Edward, Montagu surprised the world by attacking the band which beset York. He routed its vanguard, captured Huldyard, and had him beheaded.

But this engagement was far from checking the rising. In a week the whole of Yorkshire, from Tees to Humber, was up, and it soon became evident in whose interest the movement was working. New leaders appeared. Sir John Coniers, the husband of Warwick's niece, and one of the most influential Yorkists of the North, replaced Huldyard, and assumed his name of Robin of Redesdale, while with him were Henry Neville of Latimer and Lord Fitzhugh. Instead of lingering at the gates of York, the great body of insurgents—rumour made it more than thirty thousand strong—rolled southward into the Midlands. They were coming, they said, to lay their grievances before the King; and in every place that they passed they hung their articles, obviously the work of some old political hand, on the church doors.

King Edward seems to have been taken quite unawares by this dangerous insurrection. He had kept his eye on Warwick alone, and when Warwick was over-sea he thought himself safe. At the end of June he had been making a progress in Norfolk, with no force at his back save two hundred archers, a bodyguard whom he had raised in 1468 and kept always around him. Hearing of the stir in Yorkshire, he rode north-ward to Nottingham, calling in such force as could be gathered by the way. As he went, news reached him which suddenly revealed the whole scope of the insurrection.

The moment that his brother's attention was drawn off by the Northern rising, the Duke of Clarence had quietly slipped over to Calais, and with him went George Neville the Archbishop of York. This looked suspicious, and the King at once wrote to Clarence, Warwick, and the Archbishop, bidding them all come to him without delay. Long before his orders can have reached them, the tale of treason was out. Within twelve hours of Clarence's arrival at Calais the long-projected marriage between him and Isabel Neville had been celebrated, in full defiance of the King. Warwick and Clarence kept holiday but for one day; the marriage took place on the 11th, and by the 12th they were in Kent with a strong party of the garrison of Calais as their escort.

The unruly Kentishmen rose in a body in Warwick's favour, as eagerly as when they had mustered to his banner in 1460 before the battle of Northampton. The Earl and the Duke came to Canterbury with several thousand men at their back. There they revealed their treasonable intent, for they published a declaration that they considered the articles of Robin of Redesdale just and salutary, and would do their best to bring them to the King's notice. How the King was to be persuaded was indicated clearly enough, by a proclamation which summoned out the whole shire of Kent to join the Earl's banner. Warwick and his son-in-law then marched on London, which promptly threw open its gates. The King was thus caught between two fires—the open rebels lay to the north of him, his brother and cousin with their armed persuasion to the south.

Even before Warwick's treason had been known, the King had recognised the danger of the northern rising, and sent commissions of array all over England. Two considerable forces were soon in arms in his behalf. Herbert, the new Earl of Pembroke, raised fourteen thousand Welsh and Marchmen at Brecon and Ludlow, and set out eastward. Stafford, the new Earl of Devon, collected six thousand archers in the South-Western Counties, and set out northward. The King lay at Nottingham with Lord Hastings, Lord Mountjoy, and the Woodvilles. He seems to have had nearly fifteen thousand men in his company; but their spirit was bad. "Sire," said Mountjoy to him in full council of war, "no one wishes your person ill, but it would be well to send away my Lord of Rivers and his children when you have done conferring with them." Edward took this advice. Rivers and John Woodville forthwith retired to Chepstow; Scales joined his sister the Queen at Cambridge.

Meanwhile the Northern rebels were pouring south by way of Doncaster and Derby. Their leaders Coniers and Latimer showed considerable military skill, for by a rapid march on to Leicester they got between the King and Lord Herbert's army. Edward, for once out-generalled, had to follow them southward, but the Yorkshiremen were some days ahead of him, and on July 25th reached Daventry. On the same day Herbert and Stafford concentrated their forces at Banbury; but on their first meeting the two new earls fell to hard words on a private quarrel, and, although the enemy was so near, Stafford in a moment of pique drew off his six thousand men to Deddington, ten miles away, leaving Pembroke's fourteen thousand Welsh pikemen altogether unprovided with archery.

Next day all the chief actors in the scene were converging on the same spot in central England—Coniers marching from Daventry on to Banbury, Pembroke from Banbury on Daventry, with Stafford following in his rear, while Warwick and Clarence had left London and were moving by St. Albans on Towcester; the King, following the Yorkshiremen, was somewhere near Northampton.

Coniers and his colleagues, to whom belong all the honours of generalship in this campaign, once more got ahead of their opponents. Moving rapidly on Banbury on the 26th, they found Pembroke's army approaching them on a common named Danesmoor, near Edgecott Park, six miles north of Banbury. The Welsh took up a position covered by a small stream and offered battle, though they were greatly inferior in numbers. The Northerners promptly attacked them, and though one of their three leaders, Henry Neville of Latimer, fell in the first onset, gained a complete victory; "by force of archery they forced the Welsh to descend from the hill into the valley," though Herbert and his brothers did all that brave knights could to save the battle. The King was only a few hours' march away; indeed, his vanguard under Sir Geoffrey Gate and Thomas Clapham actually reached the field, but both were old officers of Warwick, and instead of falling on the rebels' rear, proceeded to join them, and led the final attack on Herbert's position.

Thunderstruck at the deep demoralisation among his troops which this desertion showed, the King fell back on Olney, abandoning Northampton to the rebels. Next day—it was July 27th—the brave Earl of Pembroke and his brother Richard Herbert, both of whom had been taken prisoners, were beheaded in the market-place by Coniers' command without sentence or trial. Their blood lies without doubt on Warwick's head, for though neither he nor Clarence was present, the rebels were obviously acting on his orders, and if he had instructed them to keep all their captives safe, they would never have presumed to slay them. Several chroniclers indeed say that Warwick and Clarence had expressly doomed Herbert for death. This slaughter was perfectly inexcusable, for Herbert had never descended to the acts of the Woodvilles; he was an honourable enemy, and Warwick had actually been reconciled to him only a year before.[12] The execution of the Herberts was not the only token of the fact that the great Earl's hand was pulling the strings all over England. His special aversions, Rivers and John Woodville, were seized a week later at Chepstow by a band of rioters—probably retainers from the Despenser estates by the Severn—and forwarded to Coventry, where they were put to death early in August. Even if Pembroke's execution was the unauthorised work of Coniers and Fitzhugh, this slaying of the Woodvilles must certainly have been Warwick's own deed. Stafford the Earl of Devon, whose desertion of the Welsh had been the principal cause of the defeat at Edgecott, fared no better than the colleague he had betrayed. He disbanded his army and fled homeward; but at Bridgewater he was seized by insurgents, retainers of the late Earl of Devon whom he had beheaded a year before, and promptly put to death.

It only remains to relate King Edward's fortunes. When the news of Edgecott fight reached his army, it disbanded for the most part, and he was left, with no great following, at Olney, whither he had fallen back on July 27th. Meanwhile Warwick and Clarence, marching from London on Northampton along the Roman road, were not far off. The news of the King's position reached their army, and George Neville the Archbishop of York, who was with the vanguard, resolved on a daring stroke. Riding up by night with a great body of horse he surrounded Olney; the King's sentinels kept bad watch, and at midnight Edward was roused by the clash of arms at his door. He found the streets full of Warwick's men, and the Archbishop waiting in his ante-chamber. The smooth prelate entered and requested him to rise and dress himself. "Then the King said he would not, for he had not yet had his rest; but the Archbishop, that false and disloyal priest, said to him a second time, 'Sire, you must rise and come to see my brother of Warwick, nor do I think that you can refuse me.' So the King, fearing worse might come to him, rose and rode off to meet his cousin of Warwick."

The Earl meanwhile had passed on to Northampton, where he met the Northern rebels on July 29th, and thanked them for the good service they had done England. There he dismissed the Kentish levies which had followed him from London, and moved on to Coventry escorted by the Yorkshiremen, many of whom must have been his own tenants. At Coventry the Archbishop, and his unwilling companion the King, overtook them. The details of the meeting of Warwick and Clarence with their captive master have not come down to us. But apparently Edward repaid the Earl's guile of the past year by an equally deceptive mask of good humour. He made no reproaches about the death of his adherents, signed everything that was required of him, and did not attempt to escape. The first batch of privy seals issued under Warwick's influence are dated from Coventry on August 2nd.

The great Earl's treacherous plans had been crowned with complete success. He had shown that half England would rise at his word; his enemies were dead; his master was in his power. Yet he found that his troubles were now beginning, instead of reaching their end. It was not merely that the whole kingdom had been thrown into a state of disturbance, and that men had commenced everywhere to settle old quarrels with the sword—the Duke of Norfolk, for example, was besieging the Paston's castle of Caistor, and the Commons of Northumberland were up in arms demanding the restoration of the Percies to their heritage. These troubles might be put down by the strong arm of Warwick; but the problem of real difficulty was to arrange a modus vivendi with the King. Edward was no coward or weakling to be frightened into good behaviour by a rising such as had just occurred. How could he help resenting with all his passionate nature the violence of which he had been the victim? His wife, too, would always be at his side; and though natural affection was not Elizabeth Woodville's strong point,[13] still she was far too ambitious and vindictive to pardon the deaths of her father and brother. Warwick knew Edward well enough to realise that for the future there could never be true confidence between them again, and that for the rest of his life he must guard his head well against his master's sword.

But the Earl was proud and self-reliant; he determined to face the danger and release the King. No other alternative was before him, save, indeed, to slay Edward and proclaim his own son-in-law, Clarence, for King. But the memory of old days spent in Edward's cause was too strong. Clarence, too, though he may have been willing enough to supplant his brother, made no open proposals to extinguish him.

Edward was over a month in his cousin's hands. Part of the time he was kept at Warwick and Coventry, but the last three weeks were spent in the Earl's northern stronghold of Middleham. The few accounts which we have of the time seem to show that the King was all smoothness and fair promises; the Earl and the Archbishop, on the other hand, were careful to make his detention as little like captivity as could be managed. He was allowed free access to every one, and permitted to go hunting three or four miles away from the castle in company with a handful of the Earl's servants. Warwick at the same time gave earnest of his adherence to the Yorkist cause by putting down two Lancastrian risings, the one in favour of the Percies, led by Robin of Holderness, the other raised by his own second-cousin, Sir Humphrey Neville, one of the elder branch, who was taken and beheaded at York.

Before releasing the King, Warwick exacted a few securities from him. The first was a general pardon to himself, Clarence, and all who had been engaged in the rising of Robin of Redesdale. The second was a grant to himself of the chamberlainship of South Wales, and the right to name the governors of Caermarthen and the other South Welsh castles. These offices had been in Herbert's hands, and the Earl had found that they cramped his own power in Glamorganshire and the South Marches. The third was the appointment as Treasurer of Sir John Langstrother, the Prior of the Hospitallers of England; he was evidently chosen as Rivers' successor, because two years before he had been elected to his place as prior in opposition to John Woodville, whom the King had endeavoured to foist on the order. The chancellorship, however, was still left in the hands of Bishop Stillington, against whom no one had a grudge; George Neville did not claim his old preferment.

By October the King was back in London, which he entered in great state, escorted by Montagu, the Archbishop Richard of Gloucester, and the Earls of Essex and Arundel. "The King himself," writes one of the Pastons that day, "hath good language of my Lords of Clarence, Warwick, and York, saying they be his best friends; but his household have other language, so that what shall hastily fall I can not say." No more, we may add, could any man in England, the King and Warwick included.

Footnotes

10. Letter of William Monipenny to Louis the Eleventh. He calls it le pays de Surfiorkshire, a cross between Suffolk and Yorkshire. But the latter must be meant, as Warwick had no interest in Suffolk, and the captain is obviously Robin of Redesdale.

11. Clarence's mother was Isabel's great aunt.

12. It is fair to say that Herbert was universally disliked; he was called the Spoiler of the Church and the Commons.

13. As witness her dealings with Richard the Third after he had murdered her sons.

Chapter 15

WARWICK FOR KING HENRY

The peace between Warwick and King Edward lasted for a period even shorter than might have been expected; seven months, from September 1469 to March 1470, was the term for which it was destined to endure. Yet while it did hold firm, all was so smooth outwardly that its rupture came as a thunderclap upon the world. Nothing, indeed, could have looked more promising for lovers of quiet times than the events of the winter of 1469-70. A Parliament ratified all the King's grants of immunity to the insurgents of the last year, and while it sat the King announced a project which promised to bind York and Neville more firmly together than ever. Edward, though now married for six years, had no son; three daughters alone were the issue of his union with Elizabeth Woodville. He now proposed to marry his eldest daughter, and heiress presumptive, to the male heir of the Nevilles, the child George, son of Montagu.[14] To make the boy's rank suitable to his prospects, Edward created him Duke of Bedford. Montagu had not joined with his brothers in the rising, and had even fought with Robin of Redesdale, so it was all the easier for the King to grant him this crowning honour.

In February Warwick was at Warwick Castle, Montagu in the North, while Clarence and King Edward lay at London. All was quiet enough, when suddenly there came news of troubles in Lincolnshire. Riotous bands, headed by Sir Robert Welles, son of Lord Willoughby and Welles, had come together, sacked the manor of a certain Sir Thomas Burgh, one of Edward's most trusted servants, and were raising the usual seditious cries about the evil government of the realm. At first nothing very dangerous seemed to be on foot. When the King sent for Willoughby, to call him to account for his son's doings, the old peer came readily enough to London to make his excuses, relying on the safe conduct which was sent him. But the riots were now swelling into a regular insurrection, and soon news came that Sir Robert Welles had called out the whole shire-force of Lincoln, mustered fifteen thousand men, and was bidding his troops to shout for King Henry. Edward at once issued commissions of array for raising an overwhelming force against the rebels. Two of the commissions were sent to Warwick and Clarence, who were bidden to collect the men of Warwickshire and Worcestershire. Their orders were dated March 7th, but before they were half carried out, the purpose for which they were issued had already been attained. Edward, taking Lord Willoughby with him as a hostage, had rushed north with one of these astonishing bursts of energy of which he was now and again capable. Leaving London on the 6th, he reached Stamford on March 11th, with the forces of the home and eastern counties at his back. On the 12th he met the rebels at Empingham near Stamford, and when Welles would not bid them disperse, beheaded his aged father Willoughby in front of his army. The Lincolnshire men fled in disgraceful rout before the fire of the King's artillery, casting off their cassocks with the colours of Welles in such haste that the fight was known as Lose-coat Field. Sir Robert was caught and beheaded at Doncaster a few days later, and the rising was at an end. On Tuesday the 21st the King reviewed his troops: "It was said that never were seen in England so many goodly men, and so well arrayed for a fight; in especial the Duke of Norfolk was worshipfully accompanied, no lord there so well." Warwick and Clarence, with a few thousand men from the shires they had been told to raise, lay that day at Chesterfield, converging, in accordance with their orders, on Lincoln.

Suddenly Edward announced to his army that he had learnt from the dying confession of Sir Robert Welles that Warwick and Clarence were implicated in the rising. Though Welles had sometimes used King Henry's name, it was now said that he had really been proposing to place Clarence on the throne, and was acting with Warwick's full approval. Edward added that he had already sent to the Duke and the Earl, bidding them come to his presence at once and unaccompanied. They had refused to come without a safe conduct, so he now proclaimed them traitors, but would grant them their lives if they would appear before him in humble and obeisant wise within a week. The army was at once directed to march on Chesterfield, but when the proclamation reached Warwick and Clarence they did not obey it, and fled for their lives.

This series of events is the most puzzling portion of the whole of Warwick's life. The chroniclers help us very little, and the only two first-hand documents which we possess are official papers drawn up by King Edward. These papers were so widely spread that we meet them repeated word for word and paragraph for paragraph even in the French writers,—with the names, of course, horribly mangled.[15] Edward said that down to the very moment of Welles' capture he had no thought but that Warwick and Clarence were serving him faithfully: it was Welles' confession, and some treasonable papers found on the person of a squire in the Duke of Clarence's livery who was slain in the pursuit, that revealed the plot to him. The second document which the King published was Welles' confession, a rambling effusion which may or may not fully represent the whole story. Why Welles should confess at all we cannot see, unless he expected to save his life thereby; and if he expected to save his life he would, of course, insert in his tale whatever names the King chose. Welles' narrative relates that all Lincolnshire was afraid that the King would visit it with vengeance for joining Robin of Redesdale last year. Excitement already prevailed, when there came to him, about February 2nd, Sir John Clare, a chaplain of the Duke of Clarence's, who asked him if Lincolnshire would be ready to rise supposing there was another trouble this year, but bade him make no stir till the Duke should send him word. Without waiting, according to his own tale, for any further communication, Welles raised all Lincolnshire, making proclamation in the King's name as well as that of the Duke of Clarence. Some days after the riots began there came to him a squire in the Duke's livery, who told him that he had provoked the King, and that great multitudes of the Commons must needs die unless they bestirred themselves. So this squire—Welles could not give his surname but only knew that he was called Walter—took over the guiding of the host till he was slain at Stamford. Moreover, one John Wright came to Lincoln, bearing a ring as token, which he said belonged to the Earl of Warwick, with a message of comfort to say that the Earl had sworn to take such part as Lincolnshire should take. "And I understand that they intended to make great risings, and as far as ever I could understand, to the intent to make the Duke of Clarence King, and so it was largely noised in our host." According to his story, Welles had never seen either Warwick or Clarence himself, and had no definite knowledge of their purpose. He only understood that the purpose was to crown Clarence; all his information came from Clare and the anonymous squire.

This is a curious tale, and suggests many doubts. If Warwick wished to act again the comedy of last year, why should he send to a county where he had no influence, to a staunch Lancastrian family (Welles' grandfather fell in Henry's cause at Towton, and his father was the Willoughby who tried to kidnap Warwick in 1460) in order to provoke a rising? And if he had planned a rising in Lincoln, why did he make no attempt to support it by calling out his own Midland and South Welsh retainers, or raising Yorkshire or Kent, where he could command the whole county? That the Earl was capable of treasonable double-dealing he had shown clearly enough in 1469. But was he capable of such insane bad management as the arrangements for Welles' insurrection show? Last year his own relatives and retainers worked the plan, and it was most accurately timed and most successfully executed. Why should he now make such a bungle?

It is, moreover, to be observed that while Welles puts everything down to Clarence in his confession, Warkworth and other chroniclers say that he bade his men shout for King Henry, and all his connections were certainly Lancastrian. Is it possible that he was trying to put the guilt off his own shoulders, and to make a bid for his life, acting on Edward's hints, when he implicated Warwick and Clarence in his guilt?

It is certainly quite in keeping with Edward's character to suppose that, finding himself at the head of a loyal and victorious army, it suddenly occurred to him that his position could be utilised to fall on Warwick and Clarence and take his revenge for the deaths of Pembroke and Rivers.

Whether this was so or not, the Duke and the Earl were most certainly caught unprepared when Edward marched on Chesterfield. They left a message that they would come to the King if he would give them a safe conduct, and fled to Manchester. Edward threw his army between them and York, where they could have raised men in abundance, and the fugitives, after vainly trying to interest Lord Stanley in their cause, doubled back on the Midlands. With a few hundred men in their train they got to Warwick, but apparently there was no time to make a stand even there. The King had sent commissions of array out all over England to trusty hands, and forces under staunch Yorkists were closing in towards the Midlands on every side. Edward calculated on having an enormous army in the field by April; he himself was coming south with quite twenty thousand victorious troops, and he had called out the whole of the levies of Shropshire, Hereford, Gloucester, Stafford, Wiltshire, Devon, Dorset, and Somerset. When he heard that Warwick was moving south, he sent to Salisbury to order quarters and provisions for forty thousand men, who would be concentrated there if the Earl tried to reach the Montacute lands in that quarter.

So unprepared was the Earl for the assault that, packing up his valuables in Warwick Castle, and taking with him his wife and his two daughters, he fled for the South Coast without waiting to be surrounded by his enemies. He quite outstripped the King, who had barely reached Salisbury when he himself was at Exeter. There the Duke and Earl seized a few ships, which they sent round to Dartmouth; more vessels were obtained in the latter place, for the whole seafaring population of England favoured the Earl. When Edward drew near, Warwick and his son-in-law went on board their hastily-extemporised fleet and put to sea. They ran along the South Coast as far as Southampton, where they made an attempt to seize a part of the royal navy, including the great ship called the Trinity, which had lain there since Scales' abortive expedition in 1469. But Scales and Howard occupied the town with a great Hampshire levy; the Earl's attack failed, and three of his ships with their crews fell into the enemy's hands. Tiptoft Earl of Worcester, "the great butcher of England," tried the captured men, and a squire named Clapham and nineteen more were hung and then impaled by him. This atrocious punishment sent a shock of horror through England, and Tiptoft's name is still remembered rather for this abomination than for all the learning and accomplishments which made him Caxton's idol.

Warwick made for Calais, where his friend Wenlock was in charge, expecting free admittance. But the King had sent Galliard de Duras and other officers across to watch the governor, and Wenlock, who was somewhat of a time-server, dared not show his heart. When Warwick appeared in the roads he refused him entry, and shot off some harmless cannon toward the ships. At the same time he sent the Earl a secret message that "he would give him a fair account of Calais upon the first opportunity, if he would betake himself to France and wait." While Warwick lay off Calais his daughter, Clarence's wife, was delivered of a son. Wenlock sent out for her use two flagons of wine, but would not give her a safe conduct to land—"a great severity for a servant to use towards his lord," remarks Commines.

Repulsed from Calais, though we hear that the majority of the garrison and inhabitants wished to admit them, Warwick and Clarence turned back, and sought refuge in the harbour of Honfleur, where they trusted to get shelter from Louis of France. On their way between Calais and Honfleur they made prizes of several ships belonging to the Duke of Burgundy, because they understood that he was arming against them. Louis kept away from Warwick for a time; but he sent his secretary, Du Plessis, to see him, and his admiral, the Bastard of Bourbon, gave the fugitives a hearty welcome. Louis was still at war with England, and still dreading a descent by King Edward on the French coast. He was delighted to learn that he could now turn Warwick, whose abilities he had learnt to respect, against his master—anything that would breed trouble in England would keep his enemy occupied at home. The King's first orders to his officers were to allow Warwick to fit out his ships, give him a supply of money, and send him off to England as quickly as possible. But the narrow seas were too well watched. Charles the Bold, irritated at Warwick's capture of his merchantmen, had collected a great fleet of seventy sail, which swept the Channel and watched the mouth of the Seine.

The enforced delay in Warwick's departure allowed time for a new idea to ripen in the French King's restless brain. Warwick had now broken hopelessly with King Edward; they could never trust each other again. Why therefore should not the Earl reconcile himself to the cause of Lancaster? No sooner was the idea formed than Louis proceeded to send for Queen Margaret out of her refuge in the duchy of Bar, and to lay his plan before her and the Earl, when they all met at Angers in the middle of July.

The scheme was at first sight revolting to both parties. There was so much blood and trouble between them that neither could stomach the proposal. If Margaret could bring herself to forget that Warwick had twice driven her out of England, and had led her husband in ignominy to the Tower, she could not pardon the man who, in his moment of wrath, had stigmatised herself as an adulteress and her son as a bastard.[16] Warwick, on the other hand, if he could forgive the plot against his own life which the Queen had hatched in 1459, could not bear to think of meeting the woman who had sent his gray-haired father to the scaffold in cold blood on the day after Wakefield. King Louis asked each party to forget their whole past careers, and sacrifice their dearest hatreds to the exigencies of the moment.

If Warwick and Queen Margaret had been left to themselves, it is most improbable that they would ever have come to an agreement. But between them Louis went busily to and fro, for his unscrupulous mind was perfectly unable to conceive that passion or sentiment could override an obvious political necessity. Gradually the two parties were brought to state their objections to the King's scheme, the first step towards the commencement of negotiations. Warwick was the first to yield; the Queen took far longer to persuade. The Earl, she said, had been the cause of all the trouble that had come on herself, her husband, and her son. She could not pardon him. Moreover, his pardon would lose her more friends than he could bring to her. Warwick's answer was straightforward. He owned all the harm he had done to her and hers. But the offence, he said, had come first from her who had plotted evil against him which he had never deserved. What he had done had been done solely in his own defence. But now the new King had broken faith with him, and he was bound to him no longer. If Margaret would forgive him, he would be true to her henceforth; and for that the King of France would be his surety. Louis gave his word, praying the Queen to pardon the Earl, to whom, he said, he was more beholden than to any other man living.[17]

The Queen so pressed, and urged beside by the counsellors of her father King Réné, agreed to pardon Warwick. Louis then broached the second point in his scheme. The new alliance, he urged, should be sealed by a marriage; the Prince of Wales was now seventeen and the Lady Anne, Warwick's younger daughter, sixteen. What match could be fairer or more hopeful?

But to this the Queen would not listen. She could find a better match for her son, she said; and she showed them a letter lately come from Edward offering him the hand of the young Princess Elizabeth.[18] Louis, however, was quietly persistent, and in the end the Queen yielded this point also. On August 4th she met Warwick in the Church of St. Mary at Angers, and there they were reconciled; the Earl swearing on a fragment of the true cross that he would cleave to King Henry's quarrel, the Queen engaging to treat the Earl as her true and faithful subject, and never to make him any reproach for deeds gone by. The Earl placed his daughter in the Queen's hands, saying that the marriage should take place only when he had won back England for King Henry, and then departed for the coast to make preparations for getting his fleet to sea.

One person alone was much vexed at the success of Louis' scheme. The Duke of Clarence had no wish to see his father-in-law reconciled to the house of Lancaster, for he had been speculating on the notion that if Warwick drove out Edward he himself would become King. But wandering exiles must take their fortune as it comes, and Clarence had to be contented with Queen Margaret's promise that his name should be inserted in the succession after that of her son, when she and her husband came to their own again. The Prince was a healthy promising lad, and the prospect offered was hopelessly remote; Clarence began to grow discontented, and to regret that he had ever placed himself under Warwick's guidance. At this juncture his brother sent him a message from England, through a lady attending on the Duchess, praying him not to wreck the fortunes of his own family by adhering to the house of Lancaster, and bidding him remember the hereditary hatred that lay between them. Edward offered his brother a full pardon. Clarence replied by promising to come over to the King so soon as he and Warwick should reach England. Of all these negotiations Warwick suspected not a word.

Edward was so overjoyed by his brother's engagement to wreck the Earl's invasion, that he laughed at Charles of Burgundy for squandering money in keeping a fleet at sea to intercept Warwick, and declared that what he most wished was to see his adversary safely landed on English soil, to be dealt with by himself.

He had his wish soon enough. In September the equinoctial gales caught the Burgundian fleet and blew it to the four winds, some of the vessels being driven as far as Scotland and Denmark. This left the coast clear for Warwick, who had long been waiting to put to sea. The Earl had already taken his precautions to make his task easy. A proclamation, signed by himself and Clarence, had been scattered all over England by willing hands. It said that the exiles were returning "to set right and justice to their places, and to reduce and redeem for ever the realm from its thraldom;" but no mention was made either of Edward or Henry in it, a curious fact which seems to point out that the Lancastrian alliance was not to be avowed till the last moment. But more useful than many proclamations was the message which the Earl sent into the North Country; he prayed his kinsman Fitzhugh to stir up Yorkshire and draw the King northward, as he had done before, when he and Coniers worked the rebellion of Robin of Redesdale.

Fitzhugh had no difficulty in rousing the Neville tenants about Middleham; and Edward, as Warwick expected, no sooner heard of this insurrection than he hurried to put it down, taking with him his brother Richard of Gloucester, Scales, Hastings, Say, and many more of his most trusted barons, with a good part of the army that was disposable to resist a landing on the South Coast. Near York he was to be met by Montagu, who had adhered to him for the past year in spite of his brother's rebellion. But the King had paid Montagu badly for his loyalty. He had taken from him the Percy lands in Northumberland, and restored them to the young heir of that ancient house, compensating, as he thought, the dispossessed Neville by making him a marquis, and handing him over some of Warwick's confiscated northern estates. Montagu complained in secret that "he had been given a marquisate, and a pie's nest to maintain it withal," and was far from being so contented as the King supposed.

On September 25th Warwick landed unopposed at Dartmouth. In his company was not only Clarence but several of the great Lancastrian lords who had been living in exile—Jasper of Pembroke, Oxford, and many more. They brought with them about two thousand men, of whom half were French archers lent by Louis. The moment that the invaders landed, Warwick and Clarence declared themselves, by putting forth a proclamation in favour of King Henry. Devon and Somerset had always been Lancastrian strongholds, and the old retainers of the Beauforts and of Exeter came in by hundreds to meet their exiled lords. In a few days Warwick had ten thousand men, and could march on London; the King was at Doncaster, and his lieutenants in the South could make no stand without him. A little later Warwick's own Midland and Wiltshire tenants joined him, the Earl of Shrewsbury raised the Severn valley in his aid, and all Western England was in his hands.

Meanwhile King Edward, who had up to this moment mismanaged his affairs most hopelessly, moved south by Doncaster and Lincoln, with Montagu and many other lords in his train. On October 6th he lay in a fortified manor near Nottingham with his bodyguard, while his army occupied all the villages round about. There, early in the morning, while he still lay in bed,

Alexander Carlisle, the chief of his minstrels, and Master Lee, his chaplain, came running into his chamber, to tell him there was treachery in his camp. Montagu and other lords were riding down the ranks of his army crying, "God save King Henry!" The men were cheering and shouting for Warwick and Lancaster, and no one was showing any signs of striking a blow for the cause of York.

Edward rose in haste, drew up his bodyguard to defend the approach of the manor where he lay, and sent scouts to know the truth of the report. They met Montagu marching against them, and fled back to say that the rumour was all too true. Then Edward with his brother Gloucester, Hastings his chamberlain, Say, and Scales, and their immediate following, took horse and fled. They reached Lynn about eight hundred strong, seized some merchantmen and two Dutch carvels which lay in the harbour, and set sail for the lands of Burgundy. Buffeted by storms and chased by Hanseatic pirates, they ran their ships ashore near Alkmaar, and sought refuge with Louis of Gruthuyse, Governor of Holland. King, lords, and archers alike had escaped with nothing but what they bore on their backs; Edward himself could only pay the master of the ship that carried him by giving him the rich gown lined with martens' fur that he had worn in his flight.

Footnotes

14. This plan, as Lingard astutely observes, may have two meanings. Either, as we said above, it was a ratification of peace with the Nevilles, or—and this is quite possible—it was intended to draw Montagu apart from his brothers, by giving him a special interest in Edward's prosperity.

15. E.g. Waurin makes Ranby Howe, the muster-place of the insurgents, into Tabihorch, and Lancashire into Lantreghier.

16. Foreign writers record that Warwick used this language to the legate Coppini in 1460.

17. All this comes from the invaluable "Manner of the dealing of the Earl of Warwick at Angiers," printed in the Chronicle of the White Rose.

18. This is a not impossible tale. Edward, fearing Warwick's alliance to the Queen, might hope to separate them by offering Margaret's son the ultimate succession to the throne. For he himself having no male heir, the crown would go with his eldest daughter Elizabeth.

Chapter 16

THE RETURN OF KING EDWARD

The expulsion of King Edward had been marvellously sudden. Within eleven days after his landing at Dartmouth Warwick was master of all England. Not a blow had been struck for the exiled King. From Calais to Berwick every man mounted the Red Rose or the Ragged Staff with real or simulated manifestations of joy. On October 6th the Earl reached London, which opened its gates with its accustomed readiness. It had only delayed its surrender in fear of a riotous band of Kentishmen, whom Sir Geoffrey Gate had gathered in the Earl's name. They had wrought such mischief in Southwark that the Londoners refused to let them in, and waited for the arrival of Warwick himself before they would formally acknowledge King Henry. Meanwhile all the partisans of York had either fled from the city or taken sanctuary. Queen Elizabeth sought refuge in the precincts of Westminster, where she was soon after delivered of a son, the first male child that had been born to King Edward.

Riding through the city Warwick came to the Tower, and found King Henry in his keeper's hands, "not worshipfully arrayed as a prince, and not so cleanly kept as should beseem his state." The Earl led him forth from the fortress,—whither he had himself conducted him, a prisoner in bonds, five years before,—arrayed him in royal robes, and brought him in state to St. Paul's, the Lord Mayor and Sheriffs, with all the Common Council, walking before him, "while all the people to right and left rejoiced with clapping of hands, and cried 'God save King Henry!'" Then the King, after returning thanks for his deliverance in the Cathedral, rode down Cheapside and took up his residence in the palace of the Bishop of London.

Henry was much broken and enfeebled by his captivity. "He sat on his throne as limp and helpless as a sack of wool," says one unfriendly chronicler. "He was a mere shadow and pretence, and what was done in his name was done without his will and knowledge." All that remained unbroken in him was his piety and his imperturbable long-suffering patience. But his weakness only made him the more fit for Warwick's purpose. His deliverance took place on the 6th, and on October 9th we find him beginning to sign a long series of documents which reconstituted the government of the realm. It was made clear from the first that Warwick and his friends were to have charge of the King rather than the Lancastrian peers. In the first batch of appointments Warwick became the King's Lieutenant, and resumed his old posts of Captain of Calais and Admiral. George Neville was restored to the Chancellorship, and Sir John Langstrother, Prior of the Hospitallers, received again the Treasury, which Warwick had bestowed on him in 1469. The Duke of Clarence was made Lieutenant of Ireland, a post he had enjoyed under his brother till his exile in 1470. Among the Lancastrians, Oxford was made Constable, and Pembroke joint-Lieutenant under Warwick. The rest received back their confiscated lands, but got no official preferment.

Oxford's first exercise of his power as Constable was to try Tiptoft Earl of Worcester, one of the few of King Edward's adherents whom no one could pardon. Oxford had to avenge on him his father and brother, whom the Earl had sentenced to be drawn and quartered in 1462, while Warwick remembered his adherents impaled in the previous April. The Butcher of England got no mercy, as might be expected, and was beheaded on October 18th.

A few days before summonses had been sent out in the King's name for a Parliament to meet on November 26th, for Warwick was eager to set himself right with the nation at the earliest opportunity. Every care was taken to show that the new rule was to be one of tolerance and amnesty. The whole of the surviving peers who had sat in Edward's last Parliament were invited to present themselves to meet King Henry—however bitter their Yorkist partizanship had been—save six only, and of these four had fled over-sea—Gloucester, Scales, Hastings, and Say.

The Parliament met and was greeted by George Neville the Chancellor with a sermon adapted to the times, on the text from Jeremiah, "Turn, O ye back-sliding children." The proceedings of the session are lost, but we know that they were mainly formal, confirming the King's appointments to offices, ratifying the agreement made between Queen Margaret and Clarence, that the latter should be declared heir to the throne failing issue to the Prince of Wales, and reversing the attainder of Somerset and Exeter and the other Lancastrian lords, who were thus able to take their seats in the Upper House.

The most important political event of the restoration, however, was the conclusion of the treaty with France, which Warwick had had so close to his heart ever since the first abortive negotiations in

1464. An embassy, headed by the Bishop of Bayeux, titular Patriarch of Jerusalem, appeared in London when Warwick's power was firmly established, and a peace for twelve years and treaty of alliance was duly concluded. Its most important feature was that it bound England to take the French King's side in the struggle with Burgundy. When he heard that Edward had been expelled and could no longer aid Charles the Bold, Louis had at once attacked the towns on the Somme, and taken Amiens and several other important places. Next spring his contest with the Duke would begin in earnest, and he was overjoyed to know that the English power would be used for his aid, by one who had a strong personal dislike to the Burgundian. Warwick at once took steps to strengthen the garrison of Calais, which was at this time entirely surrounded by the Duke's territory, and began to make preparations for a campaign in the next spring.

It is rather difficult to gauge with accuracy the feeling with which England received the restoration of King Henry. The nation, however, seems on the whole to have accepted the new government with great equanimity if with no very marked enthusiasm. The Lancastrians were of course contented, though they would have preferred to have won back their position by their own arms. Of the Yorkists it was supposed that most of the important sections held by the Earl and not by King Edward. This was certainly the case, as later events showed, with the Commons in most parts of the country, and notably in Yorkshire and Kent, which had up to this time been so strongly attached to the cause of York. There were, however, classes in which the restoration was not so well received. It was disliked by such of the Yorkist nobility as were not Nevilles. The Duke of Norfolk and all the Bourchier clan—Essex, the Archbishop, Cromwell, and Berners—had not been displeased when Warwick chastened the Queen's relatives, but had not wished to see Edward entirely deposed. Other peers, such as Grey Earl of Kent, and the Earl of Arundel, had committed themselves even more deeply to Edward's side, by allying themselves by marriage with the Woodvilles. It was gall and bitterness to all those heads of great houses to have to seek for pardon and favour from their late enemies. What, for example, must have been Norfolk's feelings when he was compelled, as the Paston records describe, to sue as humbly to the Lancastrian Earl of Oxford as his own dependents had been wont to sue to himself?

Another quarter where the restoration was taken ill was to be found among the merchants of London. The late King had been a great spender of money, and was at the moment of his exile deep in the books of many wealthy purveyors of the luxuries in which he delighted. All these debts had now become hopeless, and the unfortunate creditors were sulky and depressed. Moreover, Edward's courteous and affable manners and comely person had won him favour in the eyes of the Londoners in whose midst he habitually dwelt, and still more so, unless tradition errs, in the eyes of their wives. Few persons in the city, except declared Lancastrians, looked upon the new government with any approach to enthusiasm.

There was one individual, too, whose feelings as to the new government were likely to be of no mean importance. George of Clarence, though he had followed Warwick to London and taken a prominent part in all the incidents of the restoration, was profoundly dissatisfied with his position. Even when he had been made Lieutenant of Ireland—an office which he chose to discharge by deputy—and presented with many scores of manors, he was in no wise conciliated. He was farther from the throne as the Prince of Wales' ultimate heir than he had been in the days of his own brother's reign. Had the chance been given him, it seems likely that he would have betrayed Warwick and joined King Edward after his return to England. But events had marched too rapidly, and he had found no opportunity to strike a blow for York. During the winter of 1470-71, however, he put himself once more in communication with his brother. The correspondence was carried on through their sisters—the Duchess of Exeter on the English side of the Channel and the Duchess of Burgundy over-sea. By this means Clarence renewed his promises of help to Edward, and swore to join him, with every man that he could raise, the moment that he set foot again in England. Meanwhile Warwick had no suspicion of his son-in-law's treachery. He trusted him to the uttermost, heaped favours upon him, and even got his name joined with his own and Pembroke's as Lieutenants for King Henry in all the realm of England.

For five months the Earl's reign was undisturbed. There was no one in the country who dared dispute his will. Queen Margaret, whose presence would have been his greatest difficulty, had not yet crossed the seas. Her delay was strange. Perhaps she still dreaded putting herself in the hands of her old enemy; perhaps the King of France detained her till Warwick should have made his power in England too firm to be troubled by her intrigues. But the Earl himself actually desired her presence. He several times invited her to hasten her arrival, and at last sent over Langstrother, the Treasurer of England, to urge his suit and escort Margaret and her son across the Channel. It was not till March that she could be induced to move; and by March the time was overdue.

Meanwhile King Edward had received but a luke-warm reception at the Court of Burgundy. Duke Charles, saddled with his French war, would have preferred to keep at peace with England. His sympathies were divided between Lancaster and York. If his wife was Edward's sister, he himself had Lancastrian blood in his veins, and had long maintained Somerset, Exeter, and other Lancastrian exiles at his Court. But he was driven into taking a decided line in favour of Edward by the fact that Warwick, his personal enemy, was supreme in the counsels of England. If the Earl allied himself to Louis of France, it became absolutely necessary for Duke Charles to lend his support to his exiled brother-in-law, with the object of upsetting Warwick's domination.

Edward himself had found again his ancient restless energy in the day of adversity. He knew that in the last autumn he could have made a good defence if it had not been for Montagu's sudden treachery, and was determined not to consider his cause lost till it had been fairly tried by the arbitrament of the sword. He was in full communication with England, and had learnt that many more beside Clarence were eager to see him land. The adventure would be perilous, for he would have to fight not only, as of old, the Lancastrian party, but the vast masses of the Commons whose trust had always been in the great Earl. But peril seems to have been rather an incentive than a deterrent to Edward, when the reckless mood was on him. He took the aid that Charles of Burgundy promised, though it was given in secret and with a grudging heart. After a final interview with the Duke at Aire, he moved off in February to Flushing, where a few ships had been collected for him in the haven among the marshes of Walcheren. About fifteen hundred English refugees accompanied him, including his brother of Gloucester and Lords Hastings, Say, and Scales. The Duke had hired for him three hundred German hand-gun men, and presented him with fifty thousand florins in gold. With such slender resources the exiled King did not scruple to attempt the reconquest of his kingdom. On March 11th he and his men set sail. They were convoyed across the German Ocean by a fleet of fourteen armed Hanseatic vessels, which the Duke had sent for their protection. Yet the moment that Charles heard they were safely departed, he published, for Warwick's benefit, a proclamation warning any of his subjects against aiding or abetting Edward of York in any enterprise against the realm of England.

However secretly Edward's preparations were concerted, they had not entirely escaped his enemy's notice. Warwick had made dispositions for resisting a landing to the best of his ability. A fleet stationed at Calais, under the Bastard of Fauconbridge, watched the straits and protected the Kentish coast. The Earl himself lay at London to overawe the discontented and guard King Henry. Oxford held command in the Eastern Counties—the most dangerous district, for Norfolk and the Bourchiers were rightly suspected of keeping up communication with Edward. In the North Montagu and the Earl of Northumberland were in charge from Hull to Berwick with divided authority.

As Warwick had expected, the invaders aimed at landing in East Anglia. On March 12th Edward and his fleet lay off Cromer. He sent two knights ashore to rouse the country ere he himself set foot on land. But in a few hours the messengers returned. They bade him hoist sail again, for Oxford was keeping strict watch over all those parts, and Edward's friends were all in prison or bound over to good behaviour. On receiving this disappointing intelligence, Edward determined on one of those bold strokes which were so often his salvation. If the friendly districts were so well watched, it was likely that the counties where Warwick's interest was supreme would be less carefully secured. The King bade his pilot steer north and make for the Humber mouth, though Yorkshire was known to be devoted to the great Earl.

That night a gale from the south swept over the Wash and scattered Edward's ships far and wide. On March 15th it abated, and the vessels came to land at various points on the coast of Holderness. The King and Hastings, with five hundred men, disembarked at Ravenspur—a good omen, for this was the same spot at which Henry of Bolingbroke had commenced his victorious march on London in 1399. The other ships landed their men at neighbouring points on the coast, and by the next morning all Edward's two thousand men were safely concentrated. Their reception by the country-side was most discouraging. The people deserted their villages and drew together in great bands, as if minded to oppose the invaders. Indeed, they only needed leaders to induce them to take the offensive; but no man of mark chanced to be in Holderness. Montagu lay in the West-Riding and Northumberland in the North. A squire named Delamere, and a priest named Westerdale, the only leaders whom the men of Holderness could find, contented themselves with following the King at a distance, and with sending news of his approach to York.

A less resolute adventurer than Edward Plantagenet would probably have taken to his ships again when he found neither help nor sympathy in Yorkshire. But Edward was resolved to play out his game; the sight of the hostile country-side only made him determine to eke out the lion's hide with the fox's skin. Calling to mind the stratagem which Henry of Bolingbroke had practised in that same land seventy-two years ago, he sent messengers everywhere to announce that he came in arms not to dispossess King Henry, but only to claim his ancestral duchy of York. When he passed through towns and villages he bade his men shout for King Henry, and he himself mounted the Lancastrian badge of the ostrich feathers. In these borrowed plumes he came before the walls of York, still unmolested, but without having drawn a man to his banners. Hull, the largest town that he had approached, had resolutely closed its gates against him.

The fate of Edward's enterprise was settled before the gates of York on the morning of March 18th. He found the walls manned by the citizens in arms; but they parleyed instead of firing upon him, and when he declared that he came in peace, aspiring only to his father's dignity and possessions, he himself with sixteen persons only in his train was admitted within the gate. Then upon the cross of the high altar in the Minster he swore "that he never would again take upon himself to be King of England, nor would have done before that time, but for the exciting and stirring of the Earl of Warwick," "and thereto before all the people he cried,

'King Harry! King Harry and Prince Edward!'" Satisfied by these protestations, the men of York admitted the invaders within their walls. Edward, however, only stayed for twelve hours in York, and next morning he marched on Tadcaster.

This day was almost as critical as the last. It was five days since the landing at Ravenspur, and the news had now had time to spread. If Montagu and Northumberland were bent on loyal service to King Henry, they must now be close at hand. But the star of York was in the ascendant. Northumberland remembered at this moment rather his ancient enmity for the Nevilles than his grandfather's loyalty to Lancaster. He gathered troops indeed, but he made no attempt to march south or to intercept the invaders. It is probable that he was actually in treasonable communication with Edward, as the Lancastrian chroniclers declare. Montagu, on the other hand, collected two or three thousand men and threw himself into Pontefract, to guard the Great North Road. But Edward, instead of approaching Pontefract, moved his army on to cross-roads, which enabled him to perform a flank march round his adversary; he slept that evening at Sendal Castle, the spot where his father had spent the night before the disastrous battle of Wakefield. How Montagu came to let Edward get past him is one of the problems whose explanation will never be forthcoming. It may have been that his scouts lost sight of the enemy and missed the line of his flank march. It may equally well have been that Montagu overvalued the King's army, which was really no larger than his own, and would not fight till he should be joined by his colleague Northumberland. Some contemporary writers assert that the Marquis, remembering his old favour with the King, was loath that his hand should be the one to crush his former master. Others say that it was no scruple of ancient loyalty that moved Montagu, but that he had actually determined to desert his brother and join Edward's party. But his later behaviour renders this most unlikely.

Montagu's fatal inaction was the salvation of Edward. At Sendal he received the first encouragement which he had met since his landing. He was there in the midst of the estates of the duchy of York, and a considerable body of men joined him from among his ancestral retainers. Encouraged by this accession, he pushed on rapidly southward, and by marches of some twenty miles a day reached Doncaster on the 21st and Nottingham on the 23rd. On the way recruits began to flock in, and at Nottingham a compact body of six hundred men-at-arms, under Sir James Harrington and Sir William Parr, swelled the Yorkist ranks. Then Edward, for the first time since his landing, paused for a moment to take stock of the position of his friends and his enemies.

Meanwhile the news of his march had run like wild-fire all over England, and in every quarter men were arming for his aid or his destruction. Warwick had hoped at first that Montagu and Northumberland would stay the invader, but when he heard that Edward had slipped past, he saw that he himself must take the field. Accordingly he left London on the 22nd, and rode hastily to Warwick to call out his Midland retainers. The guard of the city and the person of King Henry was left to his brother the Archbishop. Simultaneously Somerset departed to levy troops in the South-West, and Clarence set forth to raise Gloucestershire and Wiltshire. Oxford had already taken the field, and on the 22nd lay at Lynn with four thousand men, the force that the not very numerous Lancastrians of Norfolk, Suffolk, and Cambridge could put in arms. From thence he directed his march on Newark, hoping to fall on Edward's flank somewhere near Nottingham.

At that very moment the invader had thrown off the mask he had hitherto worn. Finding himself well received and strongly reinforced, he laid aside his pretence of asking only for the duchy of York, and had himself proclaimed as King. But his position was perilous still: Warwick was gathering head in his front; Montagu was following cautiously in his rear; Oxford was about to assail his flank. The enemies must be kept apart at all hazards; so Edward, neglecting the others for the moment, turned fiercely on Oxford. He marched rapidly on Newark with some five or six thousand men. This decision and show of force frightened the Earl, who, though joined by the Duke of Exeter and Lord Bardolph, felt himself too weak to fight. When the vanguard of the Yorkists appeared, he hastily left Newark and fell back on to Stamford in much disorder.

Having thus cleared his flank, Edward turned back on Nottingham and then made for Leicester. Here he was joined by the Yorkists of the East Midlands in great numbers; of the retainers of Lord Hastings alone no less than three thousand came to him in one body.

Warwick, who lay only two short marches from the invader, was straining every nerve to get together an army. His missives ran east and west to call in all the knights of the Midlands who had ever mounted the Ragged Staff or the Red Rose. One of these letters was found in 1889, among other treasures, in the lumber room of Belvoir Castle. It was addressed to Henry Vernon, a great

Derbyshire landholder. The first part, written in a secretary's hand, runs as follows:

Right Trusty and Well-beloved—I greet you well, and desire and heartily pray you that, inasmuch as yonder man Edward, the King our sovereign lord's great enemy, rebel, and traitor, is now arrived in the north parts of this land, and coming fast on south, accompanied with Flemings, Easterlings, and Danes, not exceeding the number of two thousand persons, nor the country as he cometh not falling to him, ye will therefore, incontinent and forthwith after the sight hereof, dispose you to make toward me to Coventry with as many people defensibly arranged as ye can readily make, and that ye be with me in all haste possible, as my veray singular heart is in you, and as I may do thing [sic] to your weal or worship hereafter. And may God keep you.—Written at Warwick on March 25th.

Then in the Earl's own hand was written the post-script, appealing to Vernon's personal friendship: "Henry, I pray you fayle me not now, as ever I may do for you."

Sad to say, this urgent appeal, wellnigh the only autograph of the great Earl that we possess, seems to have failed in its purpose. Vernon preferred to watch the game, and as late as April 2nd had made no preparation to take arms for either side.

On March 28th Warwick with six thousand men advanced to Coventry, a strongly-fortified town facing Edward's line of advance. On the same day his adversary, whose forces must now have amounted to nearly ten thousand, marched southward from Leicester. Next morning Warwick and the King were in sight of each other, and a battle was expected. But the Earl was determined to wait for his reinforcements before fighting. He calculated that Montagu must soon arrive from the north, Oxford from the east, Clarence from the south-west. Accordingly he shut himself up in Coventry, and refused to risk an engagement. Edward, whose movements all through this campaign evince the most consummate generalship, promptly marched past his enemy and seized Warwick, where he made his headquarters. He then placed his army across the high road from Coventry to London, cutting off the Earl's direct communication with the capital, and waited. Like the Earl he was expecting his reinforcements.

The first force that drew near was Clarence's levy from the south-west. With seven thousand men in his ranks the Duke reached Burford on April 2nd. Next day he marched for Banbury. On the 4th Warwick received the hideous news that his son-in-law had mounted the White Rose and joined King Edward. The treason had been long meditated, and was carried out with perfect deliberation and great success. A few miles beyond Banbury Clarence's array found itself facing that of the Yorkists. Clarence bade his men shout for King Edward, and fall into the ranks of the army that confronted them. Betrayed by their leader, the men made no resistance, and allowed themselves to be enrolled in the Yorkist army.

Clarence, for very shame we must suppose, offered to obtain terms for his father-in-law. "He sent to Coventry," says a Yorkist chronicler, "offering certain good and profitable conditions to the Earl, if he would accept them. But the Earl, whether he despaired of any durable continuance of good accord betwixt the King and himself, or else willing to maintain the great oaths, pacts, and promises sworn to Queen Margaret, or else because he thought he should still have the upper hand of the King, or else led by certain persons with him, as the Earl of Oxford, who bore great malice against the King, would not suffer any manner of appointment, were it reasonable or unreasonable." He drove Clarence's messengers away, "crying that he thanked God he was himself and not that traitor Duke."

Although Oxford had joined him with four thousand men, and Montagu was approaching, Warwick still felt himself not strong enough to accept battle when Edward and Clarence drew out their army before the gates of Coventry on the morning of April 5th. He then saw them fall into column of march, and retire along the London road. Edward, having now some eighteen thousand men at his back, thought himself strong enough to strike at the capital, where his friends had been busily astir in his behalf for the last fortnight. Leaving a strong rear-guard behind, with orders to detain Warwick at all hazards, he hurried his main body along the Watling Street, and in five days covered the seventy-five miles which separated him from London.

Meanwhile Warwick had been joined by Montagu as well as by Oxford, and also received news that Somerset, with seven or eight thousand men more, was only fifty miles away. This put him in good spirits, for he counted on London holding out for a few days, and on the men of Kent rallying to his standard when he approached the Thames. He wrote in haste to his brother the Archbishop, who was guarding King Henry, that if he would maintain the city but forty-eight hours, they would crush the invading army between them. Then he left Coventry and hurried after the King, who for the next five days was always twenty miles in front of him.

But all was confusion in London. The Archbishop was not a man of war, and no soldier of repute was at his side. The Lancastrian party in the city had never been strong, and the Yorkists were now organising an insurrection. There were more than two thousand of them in the sanctuaries at Westminster and elsewhere, of whom three hundred were knights and squires. All were prepared to rise at the first signal. When news came that Edward had reached St. Albans, the Archbishop mounted King Henry on horseback and rode with him about London, adjuring the citizens to be true to him and arm in the good cause. But the sight of the frail shadow of a king, with bowed back and lack-lustre eyes, passing before them, was not likely to stir the people to enthusiasm. Only six or seven hundred armed men mustered in St. Paul's Churchyard beneath the royal banner.[19]

Such a force was obviously unequal to defending a disaffected city. Next day, when the army of Edward appeared before the walls, Urswick the Recorder of London, and certain aldermen with him, dismissed the guard at Aldersgate and let Edward in, no man withstanding them. The Archbishop of York and King Henry took refuge in the Bishop of London's palace; they were seized and sent to the Tower. George Neville obtained his pardon so easily that many accused him of treason. It seems quite possible that, when he found at the last moment that he could not raise the Londoners, he sent secretly to Edward and asked for pardon, promising to make no resistance.

The capture of London rendered King Edward's position comparatively secure. He had now the base of operations which he had up to this moment lacked, and had established himself in the midst of a population favourable to the Yorkist cause. Next day he received a great accession of strength. Bourchier Earl of Essex, his brother Archbishop Bourchier, Lord Berners, and many other consistent partisans of York, joined him with seven thousand men levied in the Eastern Counties. His army was now so strong that he might face any force which Warwick could bring up, unless the Earl should wait for the levies of the extreme North and West to join him.

On Maundy Thursday London had fallen; on Good Friday the King lay in London; on Saturday afternoon he moved out again with his army greatly strengthened and refreshed, and marched north to meet the pursuing enemy. Warwick, much retarded on his way by the rear-guard which the King had left to detain him and by the necessity of waiting for Somerset's force, had reached Dunstable on the Friday, only to learn in the evening that London was lost and his brother and King Henry captured. He pushed on, however, and swerving from the Watling Street at St. Albans threw himself eastward, with the intention, we cannot doubt, of cutting Edward's communication with the Eastern Midlands, where York was strong, by placing himself across the line of the Ermine Street. On Saturday evening his army encamped on a rising ground near Monken Hadley Church, overlooking the little town of Barnet which lay below him in the hollow. The whole force lay down in order of battle, ranged behind a line of hedges; in front of them was the heathy plateau, four hundred feet above the sea, which slopes down into the plain of Middlesex.

An hour or two after Warwick's footsore troops had taken post for the night, and long after the dusk had fallen, the alarm was raised that the Yorkists were at hand. On hearing of the Earl's approach the King had marched out of London with every man that he could raise. His vanguard beat Warwick's scouts out of the town of Barnet, and chased them back on to the main position. Having found the enemy, Edward pushed on through Barnet, climbed the slope, and ranged his men in the dark facing the hedges behind which the Earl's army lay,

much nearer than he had supposed, for he took not his ground so even in the front as he should have done, if he might better have seen them. And there they kept them still without any manner of noise or language. Both sides had guns and ordinance, but the Earl, meaning to have greatly annoyed the King, shot guns almost all the night. But it fortuned that they always overshot the King's host, and hurt them little or nought, for the King lay much nearer to them than they deemed. But the King suffered no guns to be shot on his side, or else right few, which was of great advantage to him, for thereby the Earl should have found the ground that he lay in, and levelled guns thereat.

So, with the cannon booming all night above them, the two hosts lay down in their armour to spend that miserable Easter even. Next day it was obvious that a decisive battle must occur; for the King, whose interest it was to fight at once, before Warwick could draw in his reinforcements from Kent and from the North and West, had placed himself so close to the Earl that there was no possibility of the Lancastrian host withdrawing without being observed. The morrow would settle, once for all, if the name of Richard Neville or that of Edward Plantagenet was to be all-powerful in England.

Footnotes

19. The Arrival of King Edward says "only six or seven thousand" in the printed text. This must be a scribe's blunder, being not a small number but a large one; and Waurin, who copies the Arrival verbatim, has "600 or 700."

Charles W. Oman

Chapter 17

BARNET

The Easter morning dawned dim and gray; a dense fog had rolled up from the valley, and the two hosts could see no more of each other than on the previous night. Only the dull sound of unseen multitudes told each that the other was still before them in position.

Of the two armies each, so far as we can judge, must have numbered some twenty-five thousand men. It is impossible in the conflict of evidence to say which was the stronger, but there cannot have been any great difference in force.[20] Each had drawn itself up in the normal order of a medieval army, with a central main-battle, the van and rear ranged to its right and left, and a small reserve held back behind the centre. Both sides, too, had dismounted nearly every man, according to the universal practice of the English in the fifteenth century. Even Warwick himself,—whose wont it had been to lead his first line to the charge, and then to mount and place himself at the head of the reserve, ready to deliver the final blow,—on this one occasion sent his horse to the rear and fought on foot all day. He wished to show his men that this was no common battle, but that he was risking life as well as lands and name and power in their company.

In the Earl's army Montagu and Oxford, with their men from the North and East, held the right wing; Somerset with his West-Country archery and billmen formed the centre; Warwick himself with his own Midland retainers had the left wing; with him was his old enemy Exeter,—his unwilling partner in the famous procession of 1457, his adversary at sea in the spring of 1460. Here and all down the line the old Lancastrians and the partisans of Warwick were intermixed; the Cresset of the Hollands stood hard by the Ragged Staff; the Dun Bull of Montagu and the Radiant Star of the De Veres were side by side. We cannot doubt that many a look was cast askance at new friends who had so long been old foes, and that the suspicion of possible treachery must have been present in every breast.

Edward's army was drawn up in a similar order. Richard of Gloucester commanded the right wing; he was but eighteen, but his brother had already learnt to trust much to his zeal and energy. The King himself headed Clarence's men in the centre; he was determined to keep his shifty brother at his side, lest he might repent at the eleventh hour of his treachery to his father-in-law. Hastings led the rear-battle on the left.

The armies were too close to each other to allow of maneuvering; the men rose from the muddy ground on which they had lain all night, and dressed their line where they stood. But the night had led King Edward astray; he had drawn up his host so as to overlap the Earl's extreme left, while he opposed nothing to his extreme right. Gloucester in the one army and Montagu and Oxford in the other had each the power of outflanking and turning the wing opposed to them. The first glimpse of sunlight would have revealed these facts to both armies had the day been fair; but in the dense fog neither party had perceived as yet its advantage or its danger. It was not till the lines met that they made out each other's strength and position.

Between four and five o'clock, in the first gray of the dawning, the two hosts felt their way towards each other; each side could at last descry the long line of bills and bows opposed to it, stretching right and left till it was lost in the mist. For a time the archers and the bombards of the two parties played their part; then the two lines rolled closer, and met from end to end all along Gladsmore Heath. The first shock was more favourable to Warwick than to the King. At the east end of the line, indeed, the Earl himself was outflanked by Gloucester, forced to throw back his wing, and compelled to yield ground towards his centre. But at the other end of the line the Yorkists suffered a far worse disaster; Montagu and Oxford not only turned Hastings' flank, but rolled up his line, broke it, and chased it right over the heath, and down toward Barnet town. Many of the routed troops fled as far as London ere they stopped, spreading everywhere the news that the King was slain and the cause of York undone. But the defeat of Edward's left wing had not all the effect that might have been expected. Owing to the fog it was unnoticed by the victorious right, and even by the centre, where the King and Clarence were now hard at work with Somerset, and gaining rather than losing ground. No panic spread down the line "for no man was in anything discouraged, because, saving a few that stood nearest to them, no man wist of the rout: also the other party by the same flight and chase were never the greatlier encouraged." Moreover, the victorious troops threw away their chance; instead of turning to aid his hard-pressed comrades, Oxford pursued recklessly, cutting down the flying enemy for a mile, even into the streets of Barnet. Consequently he and his men lost themselves in the fog; many were scattered; the rest collected themselves slowly, and felt their way back towards the field, guiding themselves by the din that sounded down from the hillside. Montagu appears not to have gone so far in pursuit; he must have retained part of his wing with him, and would seem to have used it to strengthen his brother's hard-pressed troops on the left.

But meanwhile King Edward himself was gaining ground in the centre; his own column, as the Yorkist chronicler delights to record, "beat and bare down all that stood in his way, and then turned to range, first on that hand and then on the other hand, and in length so beat and bare them down that nothing might stand in the sight of him and of the well-assured fellowship that attended truly upon him." Somerset, in short, was giving way; in a short time the Lancastrian centre would be broken.

At this moment, an hour after the fight had begun, Oxford and his victorious followers came once more upon the scene. Lost in the fog, they appeared, not where they might have been expected, on Edward's rear, but upon the left rear of their own centre. They must have made a vast detour in the darkness.

Now came the fatal moment of the day. Oxford's men, whose banners and armour bore the Radiant Star of the De Veres, were mistaken by their comrades for a flanking column of Yorkists. In the mist their badge had been taken for the Sun with Rays, which was King Edward's cognisance. When they came close to their friends they received a sharp volley of arrows, and were attacked by Warwick's last reserves. This mistake had the most cruel results. The old and the new Lancastrians had not been without suspicions of each other. Assailed by his own friends, Oxford thought that some one—like Grey de Ruthyn at Northampton—

had betrayed the cause. Raising the cry of treason, he and all his men fled northward from the field.[21]

The fatal cry ran down the labouring lines of Warwick's army and wrecked the whole array. The old Lancastrians made up their minds that Warwick—or at least his brother the Marquis, King Edward's ancient favourite—must have followed the example of the perjured Clarence. Many turned their arms against the Nevilles,[22] and the unfortunate Montagu was slain by his own allies in the midst of the battle. Many more fled without striking another blow; among these was Somerset, who had up to this moment fought manfully against King Edward in the centre.

Warwick's wing still held its ground, but at last the Earl saw that all was lost. His brother was slain; Exeter had been struck down at his side; Somerset and Oxford were in flight. He began to draw back toward the line of thickets and hedges which had lain behind his army. But there the fate met him that had befallen so many of his enemies, at St. Albans and Northampton, at Towton and Hexham. His heavy armour made rapid flight impossible; and in the edge of Wrotham Wood he was surrounded by the pursuing enemy, wounded, beaten down, and slain.

The plunderers stripped the fallen; but King Edward's first desire was to know if the Earl was dead. The field was carefully searched, and the corpses of Warwick and Montagu were soon found. Both were carried to London, where they were laid on the pavement of St. Paul's, stripped to the breast, and exposed three days to the public gaze, "to the intent that the people should not be abused by feigned tales, else the rumour should have been sowed about that the Earl was yet alive."

After lying three days on the stones, the bodies were given over to George Neville the Archbishop, who had them both borne to Bisham, and buried in the abbey, hard by the tombs of their father Salisbury and their ancestors the Earls of the house of Montacute. All alike were swept away, together with the roof that covered them, by the Vandalism of the Edwardian reformers, and not a trace remains of the sepulchre of the two unquiet brothers.

Thus ended Richard Neville in the forty-fourth year of his age, slain by the sword in the sixteenth year since he had first taken it up at the Battle of St. Albans. Fortune, who had so often been his friend, had at last deserted him; for no reasonable prevision could have foreseen the series of chances which ended in the disaster of Barnet. Montagu's irresolution and Clarence's treachery were not the only things that had worked against him. If the winds had not been adverse, Queen Margaret, who had been lying on the Norman coast since the first week in March, would have been in London long before Edward arrived, and could have secured the city with the three thousand men under Wenlock, Langstrother, and John Beaufort whom her fleet carried. But for five weeks the wind blew from the north and made the voyage impossible; on Good Friday only did it turn and allow the Queen to sail. It chanced that the first ship, which came to land in Portsmouth harbour the very morning of Barnet, carried among others the Countess of Warwick; at the same moment that she was setting her foot on shore her husband was striking his last blows on Gladsmore Heath. Nor was it only from France that aid was coming; there were reinforcements gathering in the North, and the Kentishmen were only waiting for a leader. Within a few days after Warwick's death the Bastard of Fauconbridge had mustered seventeen thousand men at Canterbury in King Henry's name. If Warwick could have avoided fighting, he might have doubled his army in a week, and offered the Yorkists battle under far more favourable conditions. The wrecks of the party were strong enough to face the enemy on almost equal terms at Tewkesbury, even when their head was gone. The stroke of military genius which made King Edward compel the Earl to fight, by placing his army so close that no retreat was possible from the position of Barnet, was the proximate cause of Warwick's ruin; but in all the rest of the campaign it was fortune rather than skill which fought against the Earl. His adversary played his dangerous game with courage and success; but if only ordinary luck had ruled, Edward must have failed; the odds against him were too many.

But fortune interposed and Warwick fell. For England's sake perhaps it was well that it should be so. If he had succeeded, and Edward had been driven once more from the land, we may be sure that the Wars of the Roses would have dragged on for many another year; the house of York had too many heirs and too many followers to allow of its dispossession without a long time of further trouble. The cause of Lancaster, on the other hand, was bound up in a single life; when Prince Edward fell in the Bloody Meadow, as he fled from the field of Tewkesbury, the struggle was ended perforce, for no one survived to claim his rights. Henry of Richmond, whom an unexpected chance ultimately placed on the throne, was neither in law nor in fact the real heir of the house of Lancaster. On the other hand, Warwick's success would have led, so far as we can judge, first to a continuance of civil war, then, if he had ultimately been successful in rooting out the Yorkists, to a protracted political struggle between the house of Neville and the old Lancastrian party headed by the Beauforts and probably aided by the Queen; for it is doubtful how far the marriage of Prince Edward and Anne Neville would ever have served to reconcile two such enemies as the Earl and Margaret of Anjou. If Warwick had held his own, and his abilities and his popularity combined to make it likely, his victory would have meant the domination of a family group—a form of government which no nation has endured for long. At the best, the history of the last thirty years of the fifteenth century in England would have been a tale resembling that of the days when the house of Douglas struggled with the crown of Scotland, or the Guises with the rulers of France.

Yet for Warwick as a ruler there would have been much to be said. To a king of the type of Henry the Sixth the Earl would have made a perfect minister and vicegerent, if only he could have been placed in the position without a preliminary course of bloodshed and civil war. The misfortune for England was that his lot was cast not with Henry the Sixth, but with strong-willed, hot-headed, selfish Edward the Fourth.

The two prominent features in Warwick's character which made him a leader of men, were not those which might have been expected in a man born and reared in his position. The first was an inordinate love of the activity of business; the second was a courtesy and affability which made him the friend of all men save the one class he could not brook—the "made lords," the parvenu nobility which Edward the Fourth delighted to foster.

Of these characteristics it is impossible to exaggerate the strength of the first. Warwick's ambition took the shape of a devouring love of work of all kinds. Prominent though he was as a soldier, his activity in war was only one side of his passionate desire to manage well and thoroughly everything that came to his hand. He never could cease for a moment to be busy; from the first moment when he entered into official harness in 1455 down to the day of his death, he seems hardly to have rested for a moment. The energy of his soul took him into every employment—general, admiral, governor, judge, councillor, ambassador, as the exigencies of the moment demanded; he was always moving, always busy, and never at leisure. When the details of his life are studied, the most striking point is to find how seldom he was at home, how constantly away at public service. His castles and manors saw comparatively little of him. It was not at Warwick or Amesbury, at Caerphilly or Middleham that he was habitually to be found, but in London, or Calais, or York, or on the Scotch Border. It was not that he neglected his vassals and retainers—the loyalty with which they rallied to him on every occasion is sufficient evidence to the contrary—but he preferred to be a great minister and official, not merely a great baron and feudal chief.

In this sense, then, it is most deceptive to call Warwick the Last of the Barons. Vast though his strength might be as the greatest landholder in England, it was as a statesman and administrator that he left his mark on the age. He should be thought of as the forerunner of Wolsey rather than as the successor of Robert of Belesme, or the Bohuns and Bigods. That the world remembers him as a turbulent noble is a misfortune. Such a view is only drawn from a hasty survey of the last three or four years of his life, when under desperate provocation he was driven to use for personal ends the vast feudal power that lay ready to his hand. If he had died in 1468, he would be remembered in history as an able soldier and statesman, who with singular perseverance and consistency devoted his life to consolidating England under the house of York.

After his restless activity, Warwick's most prominent characteristic was his geniality. No statesman was ever so consistently popular with the mass of the nation, through all the alternations of good and evil fortune. This popularity the Earl owed to his unswerving courtesy and affability; "he ever had the good voice of the people, because he gave them fair words, showing himself easy and familiar," says the chronicler. Wherever he was well known he was well liked. His own Yorkshire and Midland vassals, who knew him as their feudal lord, the seamen who had served under him as admiral, the Kentishmen who saw so much of him while he was captain of Calais, were all his unswerving followers down to the day of his death. The Earl's boundless generosity, the open house which he kept for all who had any claim on him, the zeal with which he pushed the fortunes of his dependents, will only partially explain his popularity. As much must be ascribed to his genial personality as to the trouble which he took to court the people. His whole career was possible because the majority of the nation not only trusted and respected but honestly liked him. This it was which explains the "king-making" of his later years. Men grew so accustomed to follow his lead that they would even acquiesce when he transferred his allegiance from King Edward to King Henry. It was not because he was the greatest landholder of England that he was able to dispose of the crown at his good will; but because, after fifteen years of public life, he had so commended himself to the majority of the nation that they were ready to follow his guidance even when he broke with all his earlier associations.

But Warwick was something more than active, genial, and popular; nothing less than first-rate abilities would have sufficed to carry him through his career. On the whole, it was as a statesman that he was most fitted to shine. His power of managing men was extraordinary; even King Louis of France, the hardest and most unemotional of men, seems to have been amenable to his influence. He was as successful with men in the mass as with individuals; he could sway a parliament or an army with equal ease to his will. How far he surpassed the majority of his contemporaries in political prescience is shown by the fact that, in spite of Yorkist traditions, he saw clearly that England must give up her ancient claims on France, and continually worked to reconcile the two countries.

In war Warwick was a commander of ability; good for all ordinary emergencies where courage and a cool head would carry him through, but not attaining the heights of military genius displayed by his pupil Edward. His battles were fought in the old English style of Edward the Third and Henry the Fifth, by lines of archery flanked by clumps of billmen and dismounted knights. He is found employing both cannon and hand-gun men, but made no decisive or novel use of either, except in the case of his siege-artillery in the campaign of 1464. Nor did he employ cavalry to any great extent; his men dismounted to fight like their grandfathers at Agincourt, although the power of horsemen had again revindicated itself on the Continent. The Earl was a cool and capable commander; he was not one of the hot-headed feudal chiefs who strove to lead every charge. It was his wont to conduct his first line to the attack and then to retire and take command of the reserve, with which he delivered his final attack in person. This caution led some contemporary critics, especially Burgundians who contrasted his conduct with the headlong valour of Charles the Rash, to throw doubts on his personal courage. The sneer was ridiculous. The man who was first into the High Street at St. Albans, who fought through the ten hours of Towton, and won a name by his victories at sea in an age when sea-fights were carried on by desperate hand-to-hand attempts to board, might afford to laugh at any such criticism. If he fell at Barnet "somewhat flying," as the Yorkist chronicler declares, he was surely right in endeavouring to save himself for another field; he knew that one lost battle would not wreck his cause, while his own life was the sole pledge of the union between the Lancastrian party and the majority of the nation.

Brave, courteous, liberal, active, and able, a generous lord to his followers, an untiring servant to the commonweal, Warwick had all that was needed to attract the homage of his contemporaries: they called him, as the Kentish ballad-monger sang, "a very noble knight, the flower of manhood." But it is only fair to record that he bore in his character the fatal marks of the two sins which distinguished the English nobles of his time. Occasionally he was reckless in blood shedding. Once in his life he descended to the use of a long and deliberate course of treason and treachery.

In the first-named sin Warwick had less to reproach himself with than most of his contemporaries. He never authorised a massacre, or broke open a sanctuary, or entrapped men by false pretences in order to put them to death. In battle, too, he always bid his men to spare the Commons. Moreover, some of his crimes of bloodshed are easily to be palliated: Mundeford and the other captains whom he beheaded at Calais had broken their oath of loyalty to him; the Bastard of Exeter, whom he executed at York, had been the prime agent in the murder of his father. The only wholly unpardonable act of the Earl was his slaying of the Woodvilles and Herberts in 1469. They had been his bitter enemies, it is true; but to avenge political rivalries with the axe, without any legal form of trial, was unworthy of the high reputation which Warwick had up to that moment enjoyed. It increases rather than lessens the sum of his guilt to say that he did not publicly order their death, but allowed them to be executed by rebels whom he had roused and might as easily have quieted.

But far worse, in a moral aspect, than the slaying of the Woodvilles and Herberts, was the course of treachery and deceit that had preceded it. That the Earl had been wantonly insulted by his thankless master in a way that would have driven even one of milder mood to desperation, we have stated elsewhere. An ideally loyal man might have borne the King's ingratitude in silent dignity, and foresworn the Court for ever: a hot-headed man might have burst out at once into open rebellion; but Warwick did neither. When his first gust of wrath had passed, he set himself to seek revenge by secret treachery. He returned to the Court, was superficially reconciled to his enemies, and bore himself as if he had forgotten his wrongs. Yet all the while he was organising an armed rising to sweep the Woodvilles and Herberts away, and to coerce the King into subjection to his will. The plan was as unwise as it was unworthy. Although Warwick's treason was for the moment entirely successful, it made any confidence between himself and his master impossible for the future. At the earliest opportunity Edward revenged himself on Warwick with the same weapons that had been used against himself, and drove the Earl into exile.

There is nothing in Warwick's subsequent reconciliation with the Lancastrians which need call up our moral indignation. It was the line of conduct which forced him into that connection that was evil, not the connection itself. There is no need to reproach him for changing his allegiance; no other course was possible to him in the circumstances. The King had cast him off, not he the King. When he transferred his loyalty to the house of Lancaster, he never swerved again. All the offers which Edward made to him after his return in 1471 were treated with contempt. Warwick was not the man to sell himself to the highest bidder.

If then Warwick was once in his life driven into treachery and bloodthirsty revenge, we must set against his crime his fifteen long years of honest and consistent service to the cause he had made his own, and remember how dire was the provocation which drove him to betray it. Counting his evil deeds of 1469-70 at their worst, he will still compare not unfavourably with any other of the leading Englishmen of his time. Even in that demoralised age his sturdy figure stands out in not unattractive colours. Born in a happier generation, his industry and perseverance, his courage and courtesy, his liberal hand and generous heart, might have made him not only the idol of his followers, but the bulwark of the commonwealth. Cast into the godless times of the Wars of the Roses, he was doomed to spend in the cause of a faction the abilities that were meant to benefit a whole nation; the selfishness, the cruelty, the political immorality of the age, left their mark on his character; his long and honourable career was at last stained by treason, and his roll of successes terminated by a crushing defeat. Even after his death his misfortune has not ended. Popular history has given him a scanty record merely as the Kingmaker or the Last of the Barons, as a selfish intriguer or a turbulent feudal chief; and for four hundred and ten years he has lacked even the doubtful honour of a biography.

Footnotes

20. The Yorkist author of the Arrival of King Edward says that his patron had only nine thousand men. But we can account for many more. Edward landed with two thousand; at least six hundred joined at Nottingham, at least three thousand at Leicester; Clarence brought seven thousand, Essex and the other Bourchiers seven thousand more. This makes nineteen thousand six hundred, and many more must have joined in small parties. On the other side Warwick had at Coventry six thousand men; Oxford met him with four thousand, Montagu with three thousand, Somerset with seven thousand, and he too must have drawn in many small, unrecorded reinforcements. The Yorkists called his army thirty thousand strong—probably overstating it by a few thousands. Their own must have been much the same.

21. Compare this with an incident at Waterloo. Ziethen's Prussian corps, coming upon the field to the left rear of the English line, took the brigade of the Prince of Saxe-Weimar for French owing to a similarity in uniform, attacked them, and slew many ere the mistake was discovered.

22. There seems no valid reason for accepting Warkworth's theory that Montagu was actually deserting to King Edward. But there is every sign that the Lancastrians imagined that he was doing so. If he had wished to betray his brother, he could have done it much better at an earlier hour in the battle.

www.ingramcontent.com/pod-product-compliance
Lightning Source LLC
Chambersburg PA
CBHW020903080526
44589CB00011B/425